CULTURES IN CONFLICT

───── 5 LESSONS ON ─────

Paul Proclaims Jesus As Lord—Part 2

DISCOVERY GUIDE

THAT THE
WORLD
MAY KNOW.

**EXPERIENCE THE BIBLE IN
HISTORICAL CONTEXT™**
Ray Vander Laan
With Stephen and Amanda Sorenson

ZONDERVAN

FOCUS
ON THE
FAMILY.

ZONDERVAN

Cultures in Conflict Discovery Guide
Copyright © 2018 by Ray Vander Laan

This title is also available as a Zondervan ebook.

Requests for information should be addressed to:
Zondervan, *3900 Sparks Dr. SE, Grand Rapids, Michigan 49546*

Focus on the Family and the accompanying logo and design are federally registered trademarks of Focus on the Family, 8605 Explorer Drive, Colorado Springs, Colorado 80920.

That the World May Know and Faith Lessons are trademarks of Focus on the Family.

ISBN 978-0-310-08590-4

All maps created by International Mapping.

All photos and artwork are courtesy of Ray Vander Laan, Paul Murphy, and Grooters Productions.

Cover design: Zondervan
Cover photography: Grooters Productions
Interior design: Denise Froehlich

First Printing April 2018 / Printed in the United States of America

CONTENTS

CONTENTS

INTRODUCTION

As a Bible teacher and study tour leader, I have had the privilege of hiking with thousands of Jesus followers in the lands of the Bible where Abraham, Ruth, David, Jesus, and Paul lived. It has been thrilling to watch group after group experience the pilgrim excitement of walking in the same places where Bible characters walked and to realize that their stories were set in real times and places. Many have returned home from places like the wilderness of the Negev desert, the ancient streets of Jerusalem, the springs of En Gedi, and the villages of Galilee with a greater hunger to know and obey God's Word.

Seeing firsthand the context in which God revealed his redemptive plan has led them to a deeper faith and understanding of God's story. It has helped them to gain an understanding of the social, geographic, and political environments of the people to whom the Text was written so they can better comprehend what the writers intended their readers to understand. It has helped them to guard against reading their own values and perceptions into the Scriptures as they seek to apply God's Word to their lives. Often they have said, "I will never read the Bible the same way again." I know their experience, for that has been my journey too.

Unfortunately, I made an assumption about understanding the Bible that turned out to be completely wrong. I knew it was helpful to study and understand the Hebrew Bible and the life of Jesus in the context of where and when particular events occurred, but I assumed that Paul, the great teacher who traveled throughout the Roman Empire, was more like a philosopher who spoke in the abstract with little awareness of the context of his audience. Then I visited the world that he was so passionate about—Ephesus, Philippi, Corinth, Athens, and Rome. And I discovered that the same experience of context that is helpful for understanding the Hebrew Bible applied to Paul's part of God's story too.

Although God's revelation is timeless and relevant to people throughout history, that revelation takes place in a cultural context—the unique circumstances and conditions—in which his people lived. Abraham cut up animals to seal a blood covenant much as the ancient Hittites did. The design of the temple of the Lord built by Solomon in Jerusalem was familiar to the neighboring cultures surrounding God's people. In Corinth where people displayed clay and marble body parts as votive offerings to the pagan god of healing, Paul described the community of faith as a body made up of many parts.[1]

God had a unique purpose for communicating his message through these culturally familiar concepts and practices that made the point of his message strikingly clear and relevant. Thus the cultural setting in which he placed his revelation is useful for not merely knowing what words mean but for understanding the message and application of the Text, much like the study of the language of ancient culture provides for the interpreter.[2] By learning how to think and approach life as the people of the Bible did, modern Christians will deepen their appreciation of God's Word.

Like the biblical writers before him, Paul communicated through the context of his world—its metaphors, manner of communication, historic events, and cultural practices—to address its problems and issues. The power and depth of his message, which was deeply rooted in the inspired Text of the Hebrew Scriptures in which he was trained, is clearly conveyed in the cultural context of the Greco-Roman world to which God's Spirit led him. His message fits that context in the same way the inspired writers of the Hebrew Text communicated God's message in the metaphors and practices of their culture. Hence, the more we know about his world, the more clearly his teaching and letters speak to us in our cultural setting. For that reason we continue our journey with Paul on his second teaching journey in the Roman province of Achaia, where he visited the great Greek cities of Athens and Corinth.

Paul's Second Teaching Tour: The Province of Achaia

Although Christians traditionally have referred to Paul's travels as "missionary" journeys, the Bible does not use that language. Paul is Jewish, so it is more likely he viewed himself as a teacher (rabbi) making disciples rather than a missionary making "converts" in the sense that Christians use the word. His mission was to present Jesus as Savior and Lord, and to invite people to believe in him and accept God's reign in their lives. Hence, to retain a Jewish flavor and communicate more clearly to a contemporary audience, I prefer to say that this study follows Paul on his second teaching journey,[3] which took him to the Roman provinces of Macedonia and Achaia that we know as Greece.

There, the gospel of Jesus confronted Hellenism, the worldview of Greek culture. These vastly different perspectives have been in conflict from the moment Satan took the form of a serpent and enticed our human ancestors with the forbidden fruit of Hellenism. At its heart, Hellenism represents the choice to "do what seems good to you" rather than to obey the commands of God our Creator, Savior, and Lord. Paul would discover that the fruit of that encounter continued to entice people in the Roman provinces of ancient Greece.

In addition, particularly in the cities of Philippi and Thessalonica, the "good news" of Imperial Rome declared the emperor to be lord and god, the one who brought peace through Roman victory. How, then, would Paul's declaration that Jesus was Messiah, Lord, and Savior sound to "Roman" ears? He was not simply presenting another god to add to the deities of the Roman pantheon. Roman emperors claimed to be divine and were referred to as "son of god," "deified one," "savior of the world," and were addressed as "lord." Roman authors and poets declared this. Inscriptions on coins, altars, statues, and temples declared this. Everywhere the results of "divine" Caesar were seen in paved roads, running water, theaters, arenas, and temples. Paul's declaration that Jesus had come as Savior, Lord, and King would imply that the ubiquitous gospel of the emperor could not be true. While he rarely confronted the kingdom of this world politically, the implications of Paul's message were clear. The conflict between the gospel of Rome and the gospel of Jesus would surface immediately.

As I walked down the *Via Egnatia*, the ancient trade route on which Paul had walked, I could imagine him, directed by the vision he had while still in Asia, walking on the same paved stones. Accompanied by a few friends,[4] he brought the good news of a different kingdom. He brought peace—*shalom* he would have called it—accomplished by the authority and sacrifice of Messiah Jesus, Lord and Savior of the world. This peace did not come by victory in war, but by *grace* through the victory of the sacrificial death of Jesus who had been executed by Imperial Rome.[5] It was not defined by economic prosperity or class status but by honoring God and serving the best interests of others. It did not come through the endless pursuit of sexual pleasure but by a restored friendship with God and others. For me, the walk on the *Via Egnatia* made a significant impression on my faith walk. It brought into focus the confrontation of worldviews that had such a great impact on that part of the world and Paul's ministry to its people.

Ardently committed to the truth that Jesus was Messiah for both Jews and Gentiles, Paul displayed superhuman energy in proclaiming and demonstrating the good news throughout the Roman world. Convinced that the time for proclaiming the good news was short, he spent several months in the province of Macedonia—the cities of Philippi, Thessalonica, and Berea. In each city, many people believed, but the political implications of his message led to life-threatening confrontation. For his safety, believers sent him on to Athens where the confrontation would be quite different.

Athens was a beautiful and sophisticated city, known for its magnificent Parthenon, recognized as the birthplace of Hellenism, and highly esteemed as the intellectual center of the Roman Empire. Its people thrived on their reputation for culture and learning, and devoted themselves to intellectual debate regarding any theological or philosophical topic. Here, Paul engaged in vigorous discussion with the Jews of the city as well as the philosophical elite. In a brilliant address to the Areopagus, he confronted the Hellenistic worldview with a presentation of the God of the Torah as the Creator and God of the universe. Although a few believed his message, most seemed bored or disinterested.

Discouraged, Paul moved on to Corinth—perhaps the most unlikely place in the Roman Empire for the message of God's story of redemption to take root. Corinth was one of the great seaports and commercial centers of the Roman world known for its lavish prosperity and extravagant self-indulgence, its reputation for drunkenness and prostitution. Sexual immorality, encouraged by worship rituals for the goddess Aphrodite, was practiced on a grand scale. The lifestyle and culture of Corinth clearly posed a significant challenge to the new believers who responded to Paul's proclamation of the gospel of Jesus.

But if followers of Jesus, transformed by the Spirit, would learn to obey God's commands for holy living, if they would live out their faith by learning to "walk as Jesus walked" in such a decadent and dark place as Corinth, they would shine as a bright light to the entire Roman Empire. They would be living

(continues on page 14)

PARTNERS IN THE MISSION OF GOD: ISRAEL, JESUS, AND JESUS' DISCIPLES[6]

	God Chooses Israel to Carry Out His Mission	Jesus Embodies Israel's Mission	Jesus' Disciples (and All Who Follow Him) Continue the Mission
Bearers of God's Image	By his grace, God created human "partners" in his own image to reflect his nature and authority. God chose Israel to be his holy people who, through their words and actions, would make him known to the pagan nations around them. To know Israel, then, was to see a glimpse of God's person and character. (Gen. 1:26–27; 9:6)	Jesus portrayed God in all his fullness in his divine nature and as the sinless image of God in his humanity. (Jn. 14:7–11; 2 Cor. 4:4–6; Col. 1:13–20)	All followers of Jesus are called to be *tselem*—the physical image bearers or representation of Jesus. We are called to be living witnesses who faithfully imitate Jesus in every life situation so that people who do not know him will glimpse the one whose image we bear. (Rom. 8:29; Col. 3:7–11; 1 Jn. 2:6)
Partners in Redemption	Commissioned to be God's "partners" in liberating creation from sin and its affects and restoring *shalom* (order, perfect harmony) to his fallen creation; to bring and be God's redemptive message so spiritually lost people outside of God's family will come to experience him as their true Lord and King. (Gen. 12:1–3; 18:18–19; 1 Chron. 17:20–24)	God's redemptive plan is founded on the sacrificial and atoning death and resurrection of Jesus—his Son, our Messiah—whose life embodied and fulfilled the mission God gave Israel. He paid the price to redeem humankind from bondage to sin. All who believe in him as Lord and Savior are redeemed and restored to relationship with God. Jesus recalled Israel to submit to God and extend his reign. (Lk. 1:68–70; 19:9–10; Jn. 3:16; 14:1–6; Rom. 3:23–26; Gal. 3:13–14; Col. 1:13–15; 1 Peter 1:18–20)	We are called to faithfully "partner" with God as his witnesses, making known by Spirit-empowered words and actions God's plan to redeem and restore our broken world. We are to seek the lost and proclaim Jesus' forgiveness of sins as the first step to being freed from bondage to sin, reconciled with God, and joining his community of redeemed people. (Mt. 10:18; Acts 1:8; 26:15–18; 1 Cor. 3:9; 1 Jn. 1:9)
Represent God's Kingdom	Israel was called to reject the kingdom of the Evil One— evident in the chaos that reigns on earth—and to extend the reign of God's kingdom—the *shalom* of life lived as God intended—by their faithful obedience to his commands. (Ex. 19:2–6)	As the Son of God, Messiah, and King, Jesus embodied the kingdom of heaven on earth. Jesus acknowledged, taught, and fought against the kingdom of the Evil One—the kingdom of this world. In his battles against Satan's kingdom, Jesus bound the "strong man" so that Satan's possessions (people bound to him) could be taken away. (Mt. 9:35–36; 12:25–29; Lk. 4:43; 11:14–22; Jn. 18:36–37)	Jesus brought the good news of God's kingdom to earth and commissioned his disciples to extend God's kingdom "on earth as it is in heaven." Proclaiming the news of God's kingdom was a key theme of John the Baptist and the disciples' message. By submitting to the will of God, followers of Jesus extend the *shalom* of God's kingdom on earth. (Mt. 3:1–3; 6:10; 9:37–38; 10:7–8; Lk. 9:1–2; Acts 8:12; 19:8)

PARTNERS IN THE MISSION OF GOD *(CONTINUED)*

	God Chooses Israel to Carry Out His Mission	Jesus Embodies Israel's Mission	Jesus' Disciples (and All Who Follow Him) Continue the Mission
Kingdom of Priests	At Mt. Sinai, God commissioned Israel to be his holy, "set apart" people—his kingdom of priests. They stood between God and all nations, displaying who God is by resisting evil and being living examples in word and deed of what God is like "in flesh." (Gen. 22:18; Ex. 7:1–2; 19:2–6; Dt. 28:9–10; 1 Chron. 16:8; Is. 2:1–4)	Jesus, high priest of a greater order than Levitical priests, was God in flesh—a living witness and a true priest who faithfully represented and displayed his Father in ways that led many in spiritual darkness to praise God. (Mt. 9:1–8; 15:29–31; Heb. 7:17–28; 9:11–15)	Jesus did not describe his followers as God's kingdom of priests in the same way as the Hebrews at Sinai, but he described their mission in the same way. Based on Jesus' instruction, Peter described followers of Jesus as a royal priesthood—God's holy coworkers who mediate his presence in the world, imitate Jesus, and live out the Word in flesh so that others will experience and praise God. (Mt. 5:16; 6:10; 1 Cor. 3:9; 1 Peter 2:4–6, 9–15; Rev. 1:4–6)
Hallow God's Name	Names in the ancient world described a person's reputation and character. To know a person's name was to know who that person really was. To "hallow" a name was to increase the reputation of the person. So Israel's mission was to increase God's "name" (reputation, honor, glory, and character) and never profane it by their unholy words or actions. By honoring God's name, God's reputation would become known among people who did not know him so that they might believe. (Ex. 20:7; Lev. 19:12; 1 Chron. 16:8; Ps.105:1; Is.12:4; Ezek. 36:20–24; 39:7; Dan. 2:47; 3:28–29; 6:19–27)	Jesus always hallowed God's name. He did nothing to profane God's name, lessen his reputation, or demean his character. Jesus lived and taught to make God's name known and draw people to the Father, which is how Jesus' disciples came to know God's very character and nature. (Mt. 6:9–10; Jn. 17:1–12, 24–26)	Jesus taught his disciples to hallow God's name by speaking and living in such a way that God would be honored and praised by others. Living unfaithfully presents a flawed picture of God and thus profanes his name. As we obediently submit to God's will and reign over all aspects of life, we make his character and reputation known so others will honor and praise God too. (Mt. 6:9–10; Acts 4:12; Rom. 15:7–10; Phil. 2:9–10; 1 Tim. 6:1)
A Light to the World	Israel's life and words were to be God's "light to the nations." They were called to fill the earth with the light and knowledge of the one true God so that those who lived in spiritual darkness might recognize his truth and be drawn to him. (1 Chron. 16:8; Is. 40:9–14; 42:5–12; 49:5–6; 60:1–3)	Jesus—"the light of the world"—brought God's true message of life and light to Israel and to the Gentiles. Fully human and fully God, he made God known, promising that those who follow him will never walk in darkness. (Lk. 2:25–32; Jn. 1:1–5; 8:12; 9:1–5; Acts 26:22–23)	Jesus taught his followers to be God's light by living righteous lives worthy of the gospel of Christ and demonstrating the good works of compassion for those who suffer so that God will be praised. This continued God's command through Isaiah that Israel was to be a light to the Gentiles. (Mt. 5:14–16; Acts 13:47–49; Eph. 5:8–11; Phil. 2:14–16)

PARTNERS IN THE MISSION OF GOD *(CONTINUED)*

	God Chooses Israel to Carry Out His Mission	Jesus Embodies Israel's Mission	Jesus' Disciples (and All Who Follow Him) Continue the Mission
Bearers of God's Presence	God's plan of redemption involved a partnership in which his people were the "bearers of his presence." God promised to live among Israel if they prepared a sanctuary—a place for his glory to dwell—first in the tabernacle and later the temple. He commanded his people to live righteously so that all nations would experience the reality and results of his presence and be drawn to him. (Ex. 25:8; Lev. 9:22–24; 2 Chron. 7:1–3)	Jesus—Immanuel (Hebrew, "God with us")—displayed God's presence far beyond the role possible for Israel. As the Son of God, Jesus brought God's presence into every interaction he had with people. Even Gentiles recognized that God was present in Jesus. (Mt. 1:23; Mk. 15:37–39; Jn. 14:6–11; 17:1–6)	Followers of Jesus are God's human "temples" in which his Spirit resides. Empowered by God's Holy Spirit, we are to live and be faithful and obedient witnesses who display God's presence and the *shalom* of his kingdom to our broken world. (Mt. 5:14–16; Acts 2:1–12, 17–18; 1 Cor. 3:16–17; Eph. 2:19–22)
God's Faithful Witnesses	Israel was redeemed and chosen to be God's witnesses to pagan nations so that all the world would know that he is God. (Is. 43:10–12)	In everything he did and everything he said, Jesus was the faithful witness of God's character and redemption. He called Israel back to God and their mission as a community of witnesses to all people so that they might know God too. (Rev. 1:5)	Just as Israel was called to be God's witnesses, Jesus called his followers to continue the mission as God's partners in his story of redemption. He taught them to be witnesses of all he had taught and done. (Mt. 10:18; 28:18–20; Acts 1:8; Rev. 1:4–7)

examples, putting on display the *shalom* of God's kingdom. So Paul did something he had not done before. He stayed in Corinth for many months, proclaiming the message of God's kingdom and teaching and training believers in the house churches to live as God's partners in redemption—one body, united in the mission of displaying God in a broken world.

The Mission of God: His Great Plan of Redemption

Paul's visit to Athens and Corinth in the Roman province of Achaia was one more step in God's plan to redeem his sin-broken world. That story began long, long ago when God's Spirit addressed the formless, empty, meaningless darkness of chaos and created a beautiful world where everything functioned as it should—*shalom* in Hebrew. As part of his creation, God made humankind in his image. He made a covenant partnership with his people to care for his creation and on his behalf to shape it toward greater fruitfulness.

But when those humans rebelled, choosing the word of the Evil One who loves chaos over the Word of their Creator, and preferring their desires over God's commands, the *shalom* of God's creation was shattered. Chaos returned, resulting in disease, broken relationships, and evil of every kind. Worse, all of humanity became separated from God, expelled from Eden where they had lived in harmony with him.

Motivated by his everlasting love for his creation, God made a plan to restore *shalom* to his fallen creation, including as his partners the very humans who had sinned against him. God would send his Son to live, die, and rise again so that sinners who have faith in him could be forgiven and restored to relationship with their Creator. Make no mistake: God's plan to restore *shalom* to the chaos of sin is founded squarely on the redemptive work of his Son, our Messiah Jesus. Nothing must diminish the foundational work of Jesus in God's story. We must also recognize that God's redemptive work not only offers eternal life to those who believe but is the basis for restoring all of God's creation to *shalom*. God chooses to use his human partners to make his plan of redemption known in the world.

For more than a millennium God had worked in partnership with people such as Abraham and Sarah, Moses and the Hebrews, Rahab, Ruth, David, Elijah, Isaiah, and many others he had called to be his witness and display the good news of his mercy to the world around them. He had entrusted his partners with his revelation and his presence. He had entrusted them with the Promised Land in order to provide for their daily bread and to give them a platform on the *Via Maris*—another trade route that served as the crossroads of the ancient world—from which to display him so that people would come to know him and accept his reign in their lives.

Wherever God reigned in the hearts and lives of his people, his kingdom would come and *shalom* would replace the chaos brought into the world through sin. Yet chaos still reigned in the world. Had God's plan failed? Was Paul's message a new way to come to know God and to participate in his peace?

The answer is no. Although God's people experienced many failures in carrying out their mission, they were not failures. God used them to prepare for the next step in his great plan to redeem and restore his broken world: the coming of Jesus, God's Son. Jesus came to fulfill a mission he alone could accomplish. His atoning death and resurrection are the only source of restored relationship with our Creator. God entrusted to his Son the very mission he had given Israel: to be the light of the world and make God's name known. [7] He revealed perfectly in word and action that God was creator of all, owner of all, and ruler of all.

Before his ascension and enthronement at God's right hand, Jesus entrusted the same mission God had given Israel—the same mission he came to fulfill—to his followers. Like Israel, followers of Jesus were to be his kingdom of priests who would put God on display and demonstrate his true nature, his great love, and his desire for all people to join his kingdom. They, too, would extend God's reign by doing his will so that his kingdom would come on earth as it already existed in heaven. They would be the light of the world, hallow his name, and make disciples by teaching others to imitate them as they imitated him. [8] They would become God's "word in flesh," demonstrating by their lives as well as their message the nature of the kingdom of heaven. [9]

So Paul and his friends walked into the Hellenistic cities of Achaia—Athens and Corinth—with the good news that God's reign was expanding and that his presence would live among those who believed the message. We will immerse ourselves in the history and culture of the Roman world in Greece as we seek to experience the story of Paul's visit. We will see how God's people—both Jew and Gentile—became living witnesses of the kingdom of heaven who put God on display in a very pagan, broken culture.

At every point those of us who have been redeemed by the blood of Jesus will be challenged to take our place, like those who have gone before us, as God's partners in that same mission. God has called and empowered us to make known by our words and actions the good news of the redeeming power of Jesus. We must join the mission. Never has there been a greater opportunity to be God's coworkers[10] who mediate his presence as a kingdom of priests and make him known to a world in darkness.

I hope the example of Paul in the Roman world of Achaia will encourage us to engage our culture as a minority,[11] seeking the welfare of the culture in which God places us. We do not have to be powerful or a majority! The early church in the world of Imperial Rome had a dramatic effect by being a faithful minority committed to carrying out God's mission to a broken world. So we must be as well.[12]

Paul: Rabbi to the Gentiles

I have heard Paul described as the first "rabbi to the Gentiles," and I like that title. It captures his commitment to the Torah as well as his God-given mission to take the good news of Messiah to people who were not Jews: the very mission God gave to Israel. In the same way God had prepared Moses before him, God uniquely prepared Paul for exactly the task he called him to accomplish— being the Jewish messenger to the Gentiles who would the message of the kingdom of heaven to the Roman world.

Paul was born about the same time as Jesus in the city of Tarsus (near the border of Turkey and Syria today), a wealthy commercial hub also known for a university equal to those in Athens and Alexandria. So for a time Paul's family lived in the social context of the wealth and philosophy—to say nothing of the morality—of the Roman world. His family experienced the rare privilege of being Roman citizens, but they were also Jews who belonged to the movement most devoted to living a righteous life in obedience to Torah—the Pharisees.[13]

When he was quite young, the family moved to Jerusalem where he experienced life in the Torah world of Jerusalem.[14] There he studied with Gamaliel, a highly respected expert on the Torah who became known as the greatest of all Jewish sages. His influence greatly shaped Paul's teaching. In fact, tradition records that

Gamaliel taught Greek wisdom so that his disciples could inter-
pret and apply the Torah to critique the philosophy and morality
of the pagan, Hellenistic worldview that dominated Roman culture. So Paul was born in the Greek world of Tarsus and brought
up in the Yeshiva of Gamaliel in Jerusalem. Plus, he was a Jew
and a freeborn Roman. That combination doesn't happen by
accident! Like Moses, Paul grew up without any idea of how God
would use him in his plan, yet he was completely prepared in
every way. The stories of Paul and Moses give great encouragement to those who become God's partners in mission.

In his own walk of faith, Paul was intensely passionate about the
Torah and its application. He vehemently opposed those who
interpreted it differently from the tradition he believed. That
zeal—whether triggered by a particular teaching of the early
followers of Jesus that he strongly objected to or the idea of
opening the kingdom of God to Gentiles who had not converted
to Judaism—likely played a part in Paul's persecution of the early
church. But then, when Paul was on his way to Damascus in
about 34 AD, Saul met Jesus.

Whatever else changed as a result of that encounter—his view
of God's kingdom, his view of the nature of Messiah, his understanding of Jesus, his view of the Gentiles—Paul's life mission
changed. He discovered that the long-awaited Messiah had come,
and the mission of being God's kingdom of priests—displaying
God in words and actions—was to extend to all nations and all
people. In a sense Paul became the "Moses" to the Gentiles—a
rabbi through whom God spoke in action and in word to lead
people out of their bondage to the pagan worldview of Imperial
Rome and into the gospel of Jesus and the *shalom* of the kingdom of God.

No longer would Paul's sole focus be on seeking to influence the
Jewish people to faithfully live out the mission God had given
them at Mount Sinai. God would use Paul, a brilliant scholar of
Torah, a man who had been trained in Greek thought and who
knew every biblical reason to keep the unclean Gentiles out of
God's kingdom, to bring the message of God's redemption to
the Gentiles! No longer would Paul fight for God's kingdom by

exerting the power of this world. He devoted himself to follow the example of Jesus, the suffering servant, who sacrificed himself for the benefit of all who would believe.

When Paul met Jesus, he did not renounce his Jewish faith or allegiance to the Hebrew Bible. In fact, he takes pride in being Jewish—circumcised on the eighth day, fluent in Hebrew, and a Pharisee of Pharisees.[15] But his understanding of God's plan of redemption changed. It was the same Bible, the same mission to the nations, the same kingdom of priests and kingdom of heaven. But the *way* God's kingdom would come had changed radically in his thinking. He realized that Jesus was the Messiah, the kingdom of God was at hand, and it came not by military conquest or deliverance but as a result of the redemptive suffering of Jesus.

Paul's journey through the great Roman cities of ancient Greece shows his commitment to God's calling on his life as a continuation of the mission God gave to Israel. Through his story we will see the Hellenistic world of the first century and the Imperial theology of a Roman colony. We will discover the exhilarating power of the kingdom of heaven in the midst of great conflict. We will thrill with God's continued desire to restore *shalom* to all things and be amazed by how he continues to use the small and the weak to bring about his great plan of redemption.

As we join Paul in his context, we should find great hope for ourselves as we continue to partner with God in the same mission his people have always had. The increasing Hellenism of our own culture will not defeat us no matter how pervasive and powerful it appears to be. Rather, as Paul wrote from a Roman prison, I pray that we will "become more confident in the Lord and dare all the more to proclaim the gospel without fear."[16] As citizens of heaven, may we live "in a manner worthy of the gospel of Christ."[17] Our mission, like Paul's, is not simply to proclaim the great commission but to step into our role as partners in God's great plan of redemption for his people from Genesis to Revelation.

Note: For additional background on Paul's life and person, see That the World May Know, Volume 15, *A Clash of Kingdoms*.

THE APOSTLE PAUL: A TIMELINE FOR HIS LIFE AND MINISTRY[1]

Birth and Rabbinic Training

6 BC   Birth of Jesus (Luke 2).

5–6 BC   Saul born in Tarsus in Cilicia to Jewish parents of the Pharisee tradition who were Roman citizens.[2]

4 BC   Family moves to Jerusalem where he was brought up (Acts 22:3).

6–30 AD   Studies "at the feet of" Gamaliel, one of the great Jewish sages (Acts 22:3).[3]

24 AD   Jesus begins teaching (Luke 3:23).

27–28 AD Jesus' crucifixion, resurrection, and ascension (Luke 22–24).

Damascus Road

30–34 AD Saul persecutes followers of Jesus (Acts 5–7, 9).

34 AD   Meets Jesus on the road to Damascus (Acts 9; Galatians 1).

35–38 AD Further preparation and training in Damascus, Arabia, Syria, Cilicia, and Jerusalem (Acts 9, 26; Galatians 1).

38–45 AD In Tarsus.

43 AD   Peter is arrested, James is executed.

44–45 AD Is discipled by Barnabas (Acts 9, 11).

First Teaching Journey

46–48 AD First teaching journey begins in Cyprus. Changes name to Paul. Goes to Antioch of Pisidia, Iconium, Lystra, Derbe (Acts 13–14).

49 AD   Emperor Claudius expels Jews from Rome.

49 AD   Jerusalem Council (Acts 15). Probably writes Galatians.

Second Teaching Journey

50 AD   Travels from Tarsus to Galatia, but Spirit would not let him go to Asia, Mysia, Bithynia. In Troas receives vision of man from Macedonia (Acts 16).

50 AD	Goes to Macedonia: Philippi, Thessalonica, Berea, Athens (Acts 16–17).
51–52 AD	In Corinth with Aquila and Priscilla for eighteen months (Acts 18).
52 AD	Returns to Jerusalem; visits Ephesus, Antioch, Galatia (Acts 18). Probably writes 1–2 Thessalonians.

Third Teaching Journey

| 54–57 AD | In Ephesus (Acts 19). Probably writes 1–2 Corinthians, Romans. |
| 57 AD | In Troas, Macedonia, Achaia for three months (Acts 20). Then in Corinth for the winter. Heads back to Jerusalem for Pentecost, traveling through Macedonia—Thessalonica, Philippi—and on to Troas and Miletus where he meets with the Ephesian elders (Acts 20). |

Arrest in Jerusalem

| 57 AD | Arrest in Jerusalem (Acts 21–23). |
| 57–59 AD | Imprisoned in Caesarea; has audiences with Herod Agrippa, Festus, Felix (Acts 23–26). |

"Fourth" Teaching Journey

| 59–61 AD | Travels toward Rome; is shipwrecked and spends winter on Malta. A prisoner in Rome for two years but continued writing and teaching (Acts 27–28). Probably writes Ephesians, Colossians, Philemon, Philippians. |
| 62–64 AD | Apparently released from prison and may have traveled to Crete, Colossae, Ephesus, Philippi, Spain, Corinth, Miletus,[4] and probably writes 1 Timothy and Titus. |

Martyrdom

| 65–68 AD | Arrested, possibly in Asia Minor, and returned to Rome. This is based on church tradition with no biblical references. Probably writes 2 Timothy. Martyred during Nero's persecution, traditionally by beheading, which was the penalty for a Roman citizen. |

ENGAGING THE MIND: PAUL IN THE STOA OF ATHENS

I remember my first visit to the legendary city of Athens like it was yesterday. I arrived at night, and my first view of the Acropolis and the beautiful temple of Athena—the Parthenon—was unforgettable. Floodlights illuminated that magnificent structure against the night sky. The beauty and power of the Parthenon standing high above the city was overwhelming. But the impact of that scene went far beyond the beauty and mystique of the Acropolis and its famous Parthenon.

For me, a seminary student at the time, Athens represented the Greek worldview of Hellenism and the self-serving political, cultural, philosophical, and religious beliefs I had been taught to recognize and resist. As the military genius Alexander the Great launched from the ports of Greece and conquered the known world, the human-centered philosophy and values born in Athens also conquered the ancient world through trade, music, language, theater, and lifestyle. Long after the military power of the Greek Empire had been dissolved by the Romans, the power of the Hellenistic worldview lived on, conquering the minds and hearts of people throughout the Roman Empire.

Being in the city that had molded the culture and people of the nations mentioned in the New Testament was a powerful experience. For the first time I realized how risky it was for the early followers of Jesus to recognize that the Greek way was not compatible with God's way, and then to make the bold choice to live a life that honored God in the midst of a Hellenistic culture. Their God-given mission—an extension of the mission of Israel and Jesus that preceded them—was to live in such a way that their every word and action would make God known to those who did not know him.

I stood at the foot of the Acropolis amazed by how the early followers of Jesus, especially those who came from the family-and-faith-focused villages of Galilee on the fringe of the Roman Empire, had any influence on the minds and hearts of people who were sold out to such a powerful and dominant culture. I was humbled by their passion, dedication, and conviction in proclaiming that God's way—not the sophisticated, wealthy, self-serving, powerful culture of the Greco-Roman world—was the way to find true peace and fulfillment in this life (*shalom*, the Jews called it). I admired Paul's *chutzpah* to stand in the heart of Athens, at the foot of the Acropolis, in the shadow of the Parthenon, and present the good news of his God—the gospel of Jesus, Messiah and King—to the intellectual and religious elite of the Greco-Roman world.

Paul's message, the good news that Jesus is Lord, had already led to upheaval in Philippi and Thessalonica because people of influence recognized it as a challenge to the emperor's claim to be Lord and God. They feared that the good news of God's kingdom would threaten the economic security of their lifestyle and their cities. But how would Paul's message be received in Athens where the intellectual elite influenced the culture of the known world? What would happen when the message of God's kingdom challenged the foundations of the Hellenistic philosophical system?

Opening Thoughts (3 minutes)

The Very Words of God

While Paul was waiting for them in Athens, he was greatly distressed to see that the city was full of idols. So he reasoned in the synagogue with both Jews and God-fearing Greeks, as well as in the marketplace day by day with those who happened to be there.

Acts 17:16–17

Think About It

When you are in a place or situation you have never experienced before—perhaps as a tourist, a new student, a new resident, or a new employee—the people, environment, and lifestyle are likely to be quite different from what you are used to.

> When you find yourself in a new and different situation or environment, how do you go about discovering the "story" of that culture and its people—what is important to their survival and well-being, how they think, what they value, and how they act and function together?
>
> What do you do, observe, and seek out in order to discover how to relate to others and function well in that new environment?

Video Notes (31 minutes)

Temples in the ancient world—meeting point of human and divine

What Paul observes about Athens

Paul presents a radical message in the Stoa

Paul receives an invitation

The Parthenon—
The dominant influence over Athens

A truly magnificent structure

A shrine to the myths of Hellenism

Video Discussion (6 minutes)

1. Many of the world's ancient temples are a marvel to us,
    even today. As you watched this video, what did you learn

about the important role temples played in the lives of people in the ancient world of the Bible?

In what ways does that realization impact your understanding of what the Bible teaches about God wanting to live among his people? About his desire to build his people into a temple that displays who he is to the world?

In what ways did the video help you to better understand the impact that Athens, a city of temples and monuments to a multitude of gods, had on Paul?

2. In ancient Greek and Roman cities, the *agora* (*forum* to the Romans) was the place where goods and ideas were exchanged. The Athenians were known for their interest in and discussion of ideas old and new. What kind of an opportunity did this present for Paul?

In what ways do you think the exchange of ideas in the
agora of Athens may have been like or unlike the ways in
which we exchange ideas in our culture?

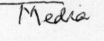
Then face to face

In terms of providing opportunities to share and
exchange ideas, what might be our equivalent to the
agora in Athens, and what leads you to that conclusion?

Media

**HAVING STOOD ABOVE THE CITY OF ATHENS FOR THOUSANDS OF YEARS THE
PARTHENON, ILLUMINATED AGAINST THE NIGHT SKY IN THIS VIEW, REMAINS AN
AWE-INSPIRING SIGHT.**

3. What impressed you most about the Parthenon, and in what ways did it inform your understanding of the thinking, values, and lifestyle of the Athenians?

4. The people of Athens devoted tremendous resources of intellect, labor, time, and money to building their temples and honoring their gods. In what ways do people today do the same?

Office Bldgs
Stadiums
Churches

What do the "temples" our culture builds as monuments to our values look like?

?

What message do those "temples" convey?

Worldly

Small Group Bible Discovery and Discussion (15 minutes)

Paul Continues the Mission in Athens

Known by some as the "Rabbi to the Gentiles," Paul took seriously his God-given mission of living and bringing the good news of God's kingdom to people who did not know God. He was totally committed to going wherever God led and sacrificing whatever was needed in order to fulfill his mission. There's no question that the path Paul walked in Greece had not been easy. In Philippi, his first stop in Macedonia, he had been thrown into jail. In Thessalonica, he had to flee the city by night in order to save his life. In Berea, where his message was carefully considered, detractors from Thessalonica soon stirred up trouble against him. For his safety, believers in Berea sent Paul to Athens.[1]

Would Paul's experience in sharing the gospel message of Jesus Christ be any different in the great city of Athens? Would the sophisticated, intellectual, idea-loving Athenians be open to hearing and accepting the good news of God's kingdom?

Paul would find Athens to be unlike any city he had visited before. It was no longer the political center of a worldwide empire, but its reputation as the intellectual and philosophical heart of the Roman world had not diminished. Amidst hundreds of monuments to Greek, Roman, Egyptian, and other gods, intellectuals and scholars from around the world gathered in Athens to display their intellectual prowess and to persuade others of the superiority of their philosophical system. Let's see what Paul discovered about Athens and its people as he prepared to share God's message with them.

1. Paul visited Athens while on his second teaching journey (Acts 15:36–18:22). He began this journey in 50 AD after the church in Jerusalem met to resolve a troublesome dispute regarding which of the Jewish lifestyle requirements Gentiles who had turned from idolatry to worship

the God of the Jews needed to follow. Accompanied by Barnabas, Silas, and other leaders, Paul delivered the official letter from the apostles and elders in Jerusalem to the believers in the synagogue in Antioch. After teaching the believers in Antioch for some time, Paul and Silas revisited the places where Paul had taught on his first teaching journey (Acts 13–14). Then, when Paul was certain of the direction God was leading, they crossed the Aegean Sea and began sharing the good news of Jesus in Greece.

Retrace their journey on the map of Paul's second teaching journey and refresh your memory of what Paul experienced in those cities.[2]

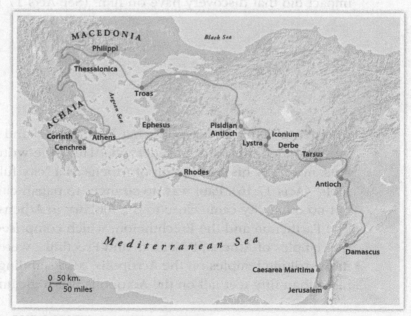

PAUL'S SECOND TEACHING JOURNEY

2. Throughout his ministry, Paul was no stranger to danger
    and risk. Read how he defends the authenticity of his
    calling and commitment in 2 Corinthians 11:22–29. Take
    note of the challenges he faced prior to coming to Ath-
    ens. Which of these trials would he likely face or avoid in
    Athens, and which new risks might he encounter when
    he presented the gospel to the most educated Gentiles in
    the Greco-Roman world?

3. Paul visited Athens under unusual circumstances, without
    his usual planning or the company of Silas and Timothy
    (Acts 17:13–15). While he was waiting for his companions
    to catch up with him, Paul began exploring the city on
    his own. What did he discover about Athens, and what
    impact did that discovery have on him? (See Acts 17:16.)

4. In order to better understand what Paul learned and how
    he responded, we must consider what Luke, the writer of
    Acts, meant by his description of Athens as a "city full of
    idols" (Acts 17:16). Paul was no stranger to pagan cities,
    but no other city came close to the idolatry in Athens.
    The Parthenon and the Erechtheion, which comprised
    the temples of Athena, Poseidon, and Erecthius, were the
    most striking temples on the Acropolis. Also standing
    more than fifty feet tall on the Acropolis was a gleaming

statue of Athena that could be seen far out to sea. In addition, temples, idols, and altars to hundreds of gods were scattered throughout the city.

In the agora were temples to Hephaestus, Apollo, Zeus, Ares, and Nike, to name a few. Temples for the worship of the imperial family, statues declaring the deity of emperors, and no less than thirteen altars dedicated to "divine" Caesar Augustus occupied the city center. In addition, every culture the Greeks encountered wanted their gods to be represented in the city too. So wherever a person looked in Athens, statues, altars, and temples to all manner of gods were in view, leading one scholar to translate Luke's description of the city as "a veritable forest of idols."[3]

a. In what ways does this picture of the spiritual environment Paul discovered in Athens differ from how you previously may have understood it?

More idols
More nations

DID YOU KNOW?
From the perspective of first-century Jewish people, idolatry was more than a religious issue. Idolatry was considered the root of evil because wherever the Lord's kingship is not recognized and another deity is honored, every kind of immorality and depravity reigns. When God's kingship is denied, there are social, political, and economic implications because idolatry, oppression of the weak, and bloodshed (especially of the innocent) all go together.

b. We know that Paul was 100 percent "sold out" to honoring God with all his heart, mind, and strength. He lived out a sacrificial commitment to display God with every fiber of his being, his every thought and action, and all of his strength so that people would come to know God. Now that we have a clearer picture of the magnitude of idolatry in Athens, where people honored every god but the God of Israel, what do you think contributed to Paul's great distress and anger (Acts 17:16)?

Considering Paul's Jewish background, rabbinic training, and his God-given mission to bring the good news of Jesus to the Gentile world, which specific characteristics of Athens might have been particularly troubling to him?

Willingness to accept every new God.

What impact do you imagine the idolatry of Athens had on Paul's view of his mission, and what impact would such an environment have had on you?

Pray for wisdom

THINK ABOUT IT
The Extreme Idolatry of Athens Provoked Paul

English translations of Acts 17:16 use terminology such as "greatly distressed," "provoked to anger," "greatly angered," "troubled," or "provoked" to describe how deeply the idolatry of Athens affected Paul. We better understand the depth of Paul's distress when we realize that the Greek word Luke used to describe Paul's response, *paroxuneto,* is the same word used in the Septuagint (the Greek translation of the Hebrew Bible) to describe God's anger with Israel when they worshiped idols:

> Then once again I fell prostrate before the Lord for forty days and forty nights; I ate no bread and drank no water, because of all the sin you had committed, doing what was evil in the Lord's sight and so arousing his anger. I feared the anger and wrath of the Lord, for he was angry enough with you to destroy you.[4]

That is a powerful anger! How might Paul's natural response to the idolatry he observed affect how he carried out his mission in Athens?

5. Most of us are unaware of the nature of idolatry and its spiritual and social impact, but Paul was a brilliant Torah scholar and rabbi who understood that idolatry goes hand in hand with immorality of all sorts. His observations of the idolatry in Athens likely reminded him of portions of the Hebrew Bible that gave him insight into the underlying attitudes, priorities, and lifestyle of the people of Athens. Read, for example, what the Text says about idolatry in Psalms 106:14, 28–29, 34–39; Ezekiel 22:1–3; 33:25–29; and Hosea 4:1–2.

    a. What kinds of evil and wickedness does the Text associate with idolatry?

b. If you, like Paul, were intent on making God known
    in a place where idolatry and the wickedness that ac-
    companies it were as dominant in the culture as was
    true in Athens, what might make fulfilling your mis-
    sion more challenging and what might make it easier?

Faith Lesson (4 minutes)

Although many years have passed since I first witnessed the
magnificent beauty and power of ancient Athens, my first impres-
sions of that city and my admiration for Paul's efforts to share
the good news of Jesus Christ with its people have not faded. In
fact, the more I have studied to understand and experience the
physical glory, intellectual sophistication, and Hellenistic lifestyle
that was Athens, the more Paul's commitment to share the gospel and extend the reign of God's kingdom in that stronghold of
idolatry amazes me.

My study also has convinced me that the culture I live in is built
on the same philosophy of Hellenism (we often call it *human-
ism*) on which life in Athens was built. That philosophy—first
declared by the serpent in the garden of Eden[5] who boldly challenged the sovereign authority of God's Word and declared that
the human mind could be like God's—values the wisdom of the
human mind above that of the Creator and the pursuit of human
pleasure above all else. I have to admit that the Hellenistic worldview of Athens has influenced my lifestyle and values just as it
shaped the lifestyle and values of the people Paul addressed in
that great city.

Yet God calls all of his people—just as he called Israel and
Paul—to be restored to his family and to take our place as partners in his great story of redemption. United into one family of

God through Jesus our Savior and Redeemer, it is our privilege to live in a broken world as examples of what God's kingdom looks like in everyday life. Our calling is to put God on display so that everyone who sees us will see what God is like and want to know him.

FOR GREATER UNDERSTANDING
What Is a Kingdom of Priests?

The Bible uses the concept of a *priesthood* to describe the mission God has given to his people (Exodus 19:3–6). In ancient times, priests would mediate between the gods and the people. This means a priest represented and acted on behalf of the god so that, by observing the priest, a person could get to know what the god was like.

At Mount Sinai, God gave his people the mission of being his "priests" to the entire world. The nature of that mission is for God's people to serve him and humanity by demonstrating God's will and character through their words and actions. God's people are not only to *bring* the message but to *be* the message in everything they think, do, and say.

In what we know as the "Great Commission" (Matthew 28:18–20), Jesus extended the mission God gave to the Hebrews at Mount Sinai to all of his followers. Thus the apostle Peter reminds followers of Jesus to this day that they are "a royal priesthood," called and commissioned to make God known to the whole earth and to live good lives that are worthy of their calling (1 Peter 2:9, 12).

So I must ask, *Do I share Paul's conviction that Jesus alone can save us from the chaos of sin? Am I passionately committed to the message that Jesus is not only Savior but Messiah, Lord, and King? Am I willing to stand up and challenge the worldview of the broken culture I live in not just by what I say but by how I live every moment of life?* I invite you to hear, experience, and learn from Paul's example as we continue this study. I invite you to commit to being a living example of God's kingdom in your family, community, and world. Are you willing?

1. How deep is your commitment to stand out in your society as a temple of the living God, a person who by word and deed faithfully puts God on display so that others will want to know him?

2. To what extent are you willing to reject the predominant worldview of Western culture with its emphasis on wealth and power, pleasure and leisure, accumulation and consumption? For example:

   In what ways do you choose to give of yourself and demonstrate compassion for the marginalized, the poor, and the oppressed rather than living for yourself at the expense of others?

   Which personal sacrifices do you make to help protect innocent life and uphold the value of every human being as an image bearer of God regardless of their ethnic background, lifestyle choices, or status in life?

   Protect unborn

Closing (1 minute)

Read 1 Peter 2:12 aloud together: "Live such good lives among the pagans that, though they accuse you of doing wrong, they may see your good deeds and glorify God on the day he visits us."

Then pray, thanking God that he made himself known to you. Ask him for the conviction, courage, and commitment to live out the message of the gospel of Jesus Christ in your world. Pray for a heart that seeks out and loves God's lost children the way he does. Seek his wisdom in sharing the good news in ways that people who do not yet know him will understand. Pray always that you will work to reclaim God's kingdom in his way by displaying how life works when God reigns. Give thanks and rejoice for every person, every inch of territory that God's kingdom reclaims from the Evil One.

Memorize

> *Live such good lives among the pagans that, though they accuse you of doing wrong, they may see your good deeds and glorify God on the day he visits us.*

> **1 Peter 2:12**

Making God Known in a Broken World

In-Depth Personal Study Sessions

Study 1 | Honoring God in a Culture of Idolatry

The Very Words of God

> *"You are my witnesses," declares the LORD, "and my servant whom I have chosen, so that you may know and believe me and understand that I am he. Before me no god was formed, nor will there be one after me. I, even I, am the LORD, and apart from me there is no savior.*
>
> *I have revealed and saved and proclaimed—I, and not some foreign god among you. You are my witnesses," declares the LORD, "that I am God."*
>
> Isaiah 43:10–12

Bible Discovery

Paul's Mission Encounters Idolatry

We live in a culture that at its core is much like the Hellenistic culture of Athens that Paul encountered there nearly two thousand years ago. Whether we realize it or not, we are to some extent willing participants in the self-serving and idolatrous ways of Hellenism. Often we put ourselves first, our wants and needs above those of others. We chase after false gods that promise to bestow honor, fame, and fortune upon us. Often we are much more concerned about the honor due *us* and how *we* can receive greater honor than we are about honoring people around us or honoring God. So it may take some effort for us to understand what it means to live in a way that brings honor to God, which is the foundation of our mission as God's witnesses to the world.

Paul, on the other hand, considered no greater responsibility, privilege, or motivation in life than to honor God so completely by his every action and word that he was an effective witness to all people that the Lord is God. When he encountered the extreme, consuming idolatry of Athens, it nearly was more than he could bear. Athens was full of witnesses to other gods. Everywhere he turned he saw honor that should have been directed toward the God of the Hebrews—the Creator of the universe— being given to idols made by human hands. In the idolatry of Athens, Paul saw clearly the conflict between the kingdom of God and the kingdom of the Evil One who does everything in his power to steal away the honor and worship that belongs to God and God alone.[6] Paul was greatly offended and angered by what he saw. The offense of idolatry in Athens caused his passion for the mission to make God known burn stronger than ever. Let's take a closer look at Paul's response to the idolatry he encountered and consider how we can become more effective witnesses who bring honor to God in the midst of our own idolatrous culture.

1. In 1 Corinthians 8:4, Paul clearly states that an idol is an image, not a god: "So then, about eating food sacrificed to idols: We know that 'An idol is nothing at all in the world' and that 'There is no God but one.'" Even though Paul declares that an idol is in itself worthless and powerless, what warnings does he reiterate from Israel's experience about the *worship* of idols? (See 1 Corinthians 10:14, 18–22; also Deuteronomy 32:15–18.)

What is at the root of all idol worship, and what does it
imply about the worshiper's life and relationship with
God as Creator and Lord?

Is it possible to be a witness who honors God and puts
his character on display in every area of life and at the
same time participate in the worship of demons? Why or
why not?

THINK ABOUT IT
Are the Gods Pagans Worship Real?

The worship of idols has been a part of human experience for thousands of
years. It is prevalent in so many cultures even to this day that we are com-
pelled to ask, "Why?" "Why is idolatry so commonplace?" "Are the 'other
gods' people worship real, or are they just a creation of our sin-distorted
minds?" How do we account for the "other gods" people worship?[7]

Although the Bible is clear that human-made images or idols in the likeness
of created beings have no life or power in themselves, it also appears to
refer to "other gods" as if they really do exist. What does this mean?

The Bible acknowledges that there is a power present in the worship of
idols. That power, of course, cannot compare with the Lord God and, in fact,
competes for recognition and honor that belongs to God and God alone.
The Bible identifies the spiritual power behind idolatry as being connected

with Satan—the Evil One—who enticed the first humans to rebel against God and thereby introduced chaos into God's perfect creation. Although the Bible does not frequently mention the connection between demonic powers and idols, it certainly is present and clearly influenced Jewish thinking on idolatry, including Paul's perspective.[8]

2. Idol worship was a significant element of everyday life in many places Paul visited during his journeys to share the good news of Jesus Christ. In his letters to the new communities of Jesus followers he left behind, Paul often warned against idolatry and encouraged believers to serve the living God and no other. What impact did Paul recognize that idol worship, and the destructive immorality that accompanied it, had on people individually and as a society? (See Romans 1:18–32; 1 Thessalonians 1:7–9.)

3. Paul was fully committed and faithful to the mission God had entrusted to his people, Israel. This is the same mission that Jesus carried out through his life on earth and entrusted to his followers to continue. That mission is about God's people living in such a way that they honor him and display his true character through their every word and action. By living righteous, God-honoring lives, God's people become his messengers and instruments of redemption who give people who do not know God the opportunity to experience him and help to restore *shalom* to the chaos of this broken world. Consider how the Text describes that mission and, in contrast, how idol worship dishonors God and violates the mission of his people.

a. What role did God intend for people, as the physical representation of his nature and character, to have in his creation? (See Genesis 1:26–28.)

What happens to the revelation of God's character and authority when his people do not represent him well, such as when they ignore their God-given responsibilities or choose to honor and worship other gods?

Chaos

b. After sin introduced chaos into God's creation, God chose the Hebrew people to be his partners in his plan of redemption and restoration of his kingdom. God's *kingdom* can be described as any circumstance in which God's will is done—any situation that demonstrates that God is reigning. God's kingdom comes as the words and actions of his people in the circumstances of everyday life bring honor to his name and display his character to the world.

At Mount Sinai, God gave his people the mission of bearing God's presence in the world so that through their witness people who did not know God would experience what he is like and accept his reign in their lives. What had God done for the Hebrew people, and what did he ask of them that would make them his "treasured possession," his "kingdom of priests," and his "holy nation?" (See Exodus 19:3–6.)

Why was the worship of idols by God's people such a great offense to him?

c. In the wilderness, where God trained the Hebrews how to live as his partners in redemption, God gave them specific instructions on how to make a place for his glorious presence to dwell among them. What did the Hebrews build, and how great was God's glory? (See Exodus 25:8; 40:33–38.)

Whose glory was on display in Athens, and, given Paul's knowledge of the Hebrew Text and God's relationship with his people, how would you expect that false representation of divine glory to affect him?

In Athens, people expended great resources to build magnificent temples and statues to display the glory of their gods. In contrast, what kind of commitment and expenditure does God ask his people to make in order to display his glory?

Our lives

d. Paul, as a Jewish rabbi, was committed to obeying all of God's commands and fulfilling the mission of extending God's kingdom in the world. So God's commands would have been in Paul's mind at all times. Read Exodus 20:1–17, which summarizes God's commands, then take a fresh look at Athens from the perspective Paul would have seen it.

What would the idolatry of Athens—not just the number of temples and worship of idols but the very foundation of Hellenism—have revealed to Paul about whose kingdom was thriving there, and why would it have troubled him?

Satan

What contrasts between God's kingdom and the kingdom of this world (the kingdom of the Evil One) would Paul have seen, and what hope would each kingdom provide for its worshipers?

In what ways does this help you to better understand why Paul, who was all about the mission, became angry about the situation in Athens, and what was the object of his anger—the idolaters or the power behind the idolatry? Why?

DID YOU KNOW?
Paul Comes to Athens with a Mission and a Message

At Mount Sinai, God commissioned the Hebrew people to be his partners in advancing his great plan of redemption by making him known to the Gentile world. Centuries later, as part of his plan to continue gathering Gentiles into the kingdom of heaven, God chose Paul to be his herald of the good news that the long-awaited Messiah had come. After meeting the resurrected Jesus on the Damascus Road, Paul eagerly accepted the same commission God gave to Paul's ancestors at Mount Sinai, the same commission Jesus gave to his disciples—to display him accurately to the world so that people of all nations would come to know him.

In fulfillment of this mission, Paul traveled throughout the Roman world preaching the gospel of Jesus and demonstrating God's love to both Jew and Gentile. He lived out the message of *kiddush ha shem* (literally to "hallow the name" by seeking to honor God and increase his reputation by everything he did) with a level of dedication and fervor rarely seen. Everywhere he went—Jerusalem, Damascus, Ephesus, Athens, Rome, or the far reaches of the Roman Empire—he proclaimed Jesus as God's anointed, the Savior and Lord of the world that the ancient Hebrew Text said he would be.

Paul's teaching was clear: the redemptive work of Messiah Jesus opened the door for all people, calling them to reject the false gods of the kingdom of this world, submit to his reign, and experience "the obedience that comes from faith."[9] He instructed all those who believed to live holy lives that would affirm the gospel and bear fruit in the hearts of a watching world.[10] His goal was not simply to provide a different religious experience, but to present Jesus—the Jewish Messiah—as the one true Savior, Lord, and King who dispelled chaos and brought the peace of the kingdom of heaven—*shalom*—to all who followed him.

4. Clearly Athens would be a battleground between the kingdom of God and the kingdom of this world. How would Paul respond? Would he stand in the agora and condemn the people of Athens? Would he throw up his hands and move on to the next city, writing off "those people" who were so immersed in the sin of idolatry? Not at all. Paul knew his calling and mission, and he would be faithful to obey God. What does Acts 17:17 say he did next, and is it what you expected? Why or why not?

5. Paul's visit to the synagogue in Athens was typical of how he began sharing the gospel in other cities he visited. As followers of Jesus today, we often lack an appreciation for Israel's role as God's witnesses and bearers of his presence in the world. But 1 Chronicles 16:8–14, 23–31 gives us a picture of Israel's understanding of their mission to make God known in their world. What do you realize from this psalm of praise about how faithful Jews understood their role as God's partners in the mission of extending his kingdom and restoring *shalom* to all people?

Reflection

In his wonderful treatment of idolatry in relationship to the mission of God, Christopher Wright identifies what drives people to create gods—idols for themselves—whether they be statues of wood or stone as in ancient times or the self-serving pursuits that people today choose in place of the living God.[11] The Bible identifies the gods of the nations as beings that were believed to provide what people desired or to protect them from what they feared.[12] So pagans worshiped gods that promoted sexuality and promised fertility because people found those things to be enticing and necessary. They also worshiped gods that promised protection from plague, enemies, storms, disease, and death.

The idols of our own experience, while more subtle, do the same. We devote ourselves to the pursuit of satisfying our basic human needs by serving the gods of gluttony or promiscuity, or we prostitute ourselves in lustful pursuit of the gods of power, pleasure, leisure, and wealth. Whether our idols are statues and images or simply the things we pursue above all else, they deny that God alone provides for our every need and satisfies our deepest longings. Idolatry robs God of the honor that is due him as our Creator who faithfully loves and provides for us.

Yet God longs for each of his children to know him and receive his gift of *shalom*. He wants every one of his children to know that, as James 1:17 says, "Every good and perfect gift is from above, coming down from the Father. . . ." In God's unfailing effort to restore *shalom* to his children who do not know him, he raised up a people to be his partners in redemption. Read Isaiah 42:6–8 and notice the compassion and love God wants to extend through the witness of those who accept the mission and follow him faithfully:

> I, the LORD, have called you in righteousness; I will take hold of your hand.
> I will keep you and will make you to be a covenant for the people and a light for the Gentiles, to open eyes that are blind, to free captives from prison and to release from the dungeon those who sit in darkness.

JOB TO ISRAEL

> I am the LORD; that is my name! I will not yield my glory to
> another or my praise to idols.

This is the heart of the mission for Paul and every follower of
Jesus. Idolatry of any sort opposes the mission of God. Will we
accept God's invitation to be partners in his great story of restoring *shalom* to a world in chaos? Will we be faithful to our God-
given mission, or will we serve idols of our own making that
steal away the honor that rightfully belongs to God?

If we want to be faithful witnesses of the gospel—faithful representatives of God's character—then we must ask ourselves some
hard questions.

> What are the idols in our own lives that claim honor and
> credit that rightfully belong to God? For example, in what
> ways does the way we think and talk about ourselves betray
> a subtle idolatry, such as when we say "I" got a job, "I" sur-
> vived cancer, "I" developed a successful business when the
> truth is God is the one who provides, heals, and blesses?

> How willing are we to release our idolatry of self and give to
> God all the honor and praise he deserves?

> In what subtle ways do we attempt to satisfy our needs and
> desires rather than trusting in God to provide?

What are the consequences to ourselves and the fulfillment of our God-given mission when we limit our knowledge and experience of God by living as if we are in charge, as if we are the gods who do it all?

How willing are we to take what we consider to be a risk and trust God to provide and bless us to his glory in order to demonstrate that he alone is God?

Study 2 | Built to Impress: The Temples of Athens

The Very Words of God

> *As you come to him, the living Stone—rejected by humans but chosen by God and precious to him—you also, like living stones, are being built into a spiritual house to be a holy priesthood, offering spiritual sacrifices acceptable to God through Jesus Christ. . . But you are a chosen people, a royal priesthood, a holy nation, God's special possession, that you may declare the praises of him who called you out of darkness into his wonderful light.*

> *1 Peter 2:4–5, 9*

Bible Discovery

God Is Building a Temple Too

The magnificent temples of Athens were an awe-inspiring display of honor for the gods who were worshiped there. Impressively beautiful temples, idols, statues, and altars located throughout the city sent a clear message of what the Athenians believed to be most important and worthy of value. Yet Paul knew that even the crown jewel of temples, the Parthenon, was a shrine to a broken world. How could he communicate that another God, a living god, also was building his temple in Athens? How could his message be heard over the influence of the temples already there?

Angered by the idol worship of the Athenians, Paul sought out the people he knew God had put in place to be his witnesses. He went to the Jewish synagogue. In that community he expected to find people whose life and words put the living God on display to a world in chaos, people who showed what life looks like when God's kingdom reigns. Among God's people Paul likely hoped to offer and receive encouragement for their mission as God's partners in redemption.

In every pagan city Paul visited previously in Greece, he discovered that God had witnesses in place who prepared the way for the good news that Jesus the Messiah had come. In every synagogue he entered he met faithful, God-honoring Jews as well as Gentiles who had been attracted to the God of Israel and had turned away from idols to serve him. God was indeed building a "temple" of his people who put him on display for all the world to see. Would that be true in Athens, the famous center of idolatry and godless human wisdom?

FOR GREATER UNDERSTANDING:
The Temple of Hephaestus

Situated on the northwest side of the agora of ancient Athens, this Doric style temple built in the fifth century BC honored Hephaestus, god of metalworkers, and Athena, goddess of craftsmen. Built of marble, it is the most well preserved of all the temples that existed when Paul visited Athens. Although it is significantly smaller than the Parthenon nearby, it has the same style and design and follows the same geometric principals. Hence, it gives a glimpse of the glory of the Parthenon when it was intact. Its beauty and grace helps modern visitors understand the strong reaction Paul had to the overwhelming dominance of idolatry he encountered when he visited Athens.

1. The challenge Paul faced in Athens was overwhelming, but he knew his calling and that of his ancestral people. What hope and mission did he share in common with the Jewish community in Athens? (See Exodus 19:5–6; Isaiah 43:10–12; Acts 26:4–7; Romans 3:1–2.)

How might their shared identity and purpose have encouraged Paul as well as the Jewish congregation in Athens?

2. Paul also knew the Text. He was well-versed in the knowledge of God's people who were faithful to their mission and, like a temple, had put God on display to the pagan world around them. As you read each of the following passages, what do you discover about the different ways people came to know God through the faithful witness of his people? (See Exodus 18:7–12; Joshua 2:1–14; Ruth 1:15–18; 2 Kings 5:6–15; Daniel 6:3–5, 11–23, 25–27.)

What can be the impact of God's *shalom* when people come to know him?

In what ways might these examples have encouraged Paul as well as the Jewish congregation in Athens? In what ways do they encourage you?

DID YOU KNOW?
God Prepared the Way for the Gospel Message

As idolatrous as the Roman Empire was, God had been at work in many ways preparing its people to receive the good news of Messiah's coming. Some of these preparations had been in place for centuries. Consider, for example, the presence of Jewish communities in nearly every major city of the empire. Some of these communities were established between 740–722 BC as a result of the dispersion of captives by the Assyrians following their conquest of the Northern Kingdom of Israel. Other communities resulted from Babylon's conquest of Judah in 586–587 BC. Still other communities were established by refugees from these conflicts and Jewish merchants who traded in cities throughout the Mediterranean world.

These communities of Jews were—in effect—God's temple, a light to the nations that displayed the Lord alone as God. In an idolatrous and class-oriented society, the Jewish communities became known for their devotion to the Text and righteous living in obedience to God's laws. By the first century, a number of Gentiles, especially women, had been drawn to the Jewish faith communities where they worshiped the God of the Hebrews and learned the teachings of the Torah. The worship practices of the Jewish synagogues ensured a biblically literate audience—of both Jews and God-fearing Gentiles—that would understand the message of the long-awaited Messiah. Furthermore, the Jewish faith was a legal religion in the eyes of Rome. This allowed early followers of Jesus, who were considered by Rome to be a part of the Jewish community, to receive the protective coverage of legal status throughout the Roman Empire.

3. Even in Athens, where idolatry played a dominant role in every part of life, God had been at work preparing the Roman world for the "good news" that Jesus the Messiah had come. What had the Jewish communities throughout the Roman Empire, including Athens, been doing that

helped to make God and his kingdom known? (See Acts
15:21.)

4. Whenever Paul visited a new city, he typically went to
    the Jewish synagogue first. What response to the gospel
    message did Paul find in each of the synagogues he had
    visited in Greece? For each community of religious Jews,
    take note of the size of the community, the influence of
    the synagogue congregation in the community, who else
    worshiped God with the Jewish congregation, and their
    response to the good news of Jesus that Paul brought.
    What does this indicate about the faithfulness of God's
    people to their mission and the "temple" God was build-
    ing in Greece?

Greek City	Philippi	Thessalonica	Berea
The Text	Acts 16:13–15	Acts 17:1–4	Acts 17:10–12
Size of Jewish Community			
Influence of Jewish Community			
Who Else Worshiped in Synagogue			
Response to the Good News			

DATA FILE
Who Are the God-Fearers?

Many accounts of Paul teaching the gospel in the book of Acts mention God-fearers, God-fearing Gentiles, God-worshipers, or God-fearing Greeks. These people were Gentiles who were attracted to the Jewish God and participated in the worship and life of their local Jewish synagogue community. Although there was disagreement within the Jewish (and, later, the early Christian) communities as to how much of the Torah God-fearing Gentiles were required to observe—whether or not they must practice circumcision, wear tassels, obey purity rituals, and follow a kosher diet—there is no doubt that they actively participated in the community of God's people. They knew the Hebrew Bible, had renounced their pagan gods and sinful lifestyle, and became a natural gateway for the gospel into the Gentile world.

Several inscriptions referring to God-fearers among the Jewish community have been found in the ruins of Miletus and Sardis in Asia Minor (present-day Turkey). The clearest evidence of their association is found on a *stele*, a marble pillar, in Aphrodisias. This pillar has legible inscriptions (in Greek) on two of its four faces[13] that relate to a charitable undertaking of the synagogue community.

The lists on the *stele* are intriguing. Scholars are quite certain that one face of the pillar (left side, left photo) lists individuals who contributed to the construction of a new building, most likely a soup kitchen or food pantry. The other face (right side, left photo) has two lists of people associated with the project. The first group of fifty-five names (some Greek, others Hebrew) are under the heading "Jews." This list also designates three proselytes or converts, meaning three Gentiles who had fully converted to Judaism (including circumcision). The second group (right photo) is under the heading *theosebes*, which means God-fearers. These apparently were Gentiles who had been attracted to God by the faithful living of the Jewish community and, although they did not completely convert to Judaism, had abandoned their pagan gods and practices to identify with the Jewish community and their God.

The *stele* is significant because it provides archaeological evidence of

LEFT PHOTO SHOWS *STELE* WITH LISTS OF NAMES OF PARTICIPANTS IN THE SYNAGOGUE'S CHARITABLE UNDERTAKING. RIGHT PHOTO HIGHLIGHTS *OSOI THEOSEBIS*.

communities described in both New Testament and Jewish sources. Even before the Christian message came to the Roman world, God had been building the "temple" of his people and drawing pagan Gentiles to himself! Wherever the early followers of Jesus went, they found people of the Text who eagerly accepted the good news that Jesus, the long-awaited Messiah, had come.

To see the pillar at Aphrodisias with its list of God-fearers is to see passionate devotion to God in action. How could any of these witnesses have imagined that their faith in God would speak not only to their world but still speak powerfully today? We can find great encouragement in the fact that if we live faithfully and speak clearly of our love for Jesus, God has and is always preparing an audience that is eager to hear the good news.

5. What did Paul find when he visited the Jewish synagogue in Athens? (See Acts 17:17.)

Given the idolatry Paul had seen in Athens, what does this reveal about the witness of the Jews who lived there?

Would you have expected the temple of God's people to be more or less influential than it appears, and why?

6. Luke's account makes a connection between Paul's distress over the idolatry in Athens and his visit to the synagogue. So, what did Paul do when he visited with those in the synagogue, and what do you think they might have discussed? (See Acts 17:17.)

7. Despite the overshadowing presence of temples and idols
    to all manner of gods, what action did Paul take to estab-
    lish a "temple" of God's presence in Athens? (See Acts
    17:17.)

Reflection

God was building his temple in Athens as well as in the other
cities Paul had visited. In the Jewish congregation, Paul found
Gentiles who had seen the "temple" of God's people and been so
impressed by the *shalom* they found there that they turned away
from the idols they worshiped in order to know and serve the
God of the Jews. So even in Athens God was building a temple,
however small, that attracted worshipers to him. But the situation
in Athens was very troubling to Paul. God's temple didn't exactly
stand out in that "forest of idols."

The NIV translation says that Paul "reasoned" with those in the
synagogue in Athens (Acts 17:17), but that terminology can be
misunderstood. In the context of understanding the Scriptures
in the Jewish synagogue, reasoning can include vigorous disagreement. The language of some other translations reflects this
stronger meaning. The King James Version translates the verb as
"disputed," and the New Revised Standard Version uses "argued."

So what was the subject of such intense discussion? The disagreement could have been about Paul's mission to share the
good news that Jesus was the promised Messiah. That had been
a point of disagreement in some synagogues. But Luke's connection between the idolatry of Athens and Paul's engagement with
the synagogue congregation opens another possibility. Perhaps
Paul was upset because so few Athenians seem to have known
and experienced the true and living God that he challenged the
congregation to live out their faith more boldly. Perhaps the

proliferation of idols in Athens had been so overwhelming to God's people that—even though they had made God known to a few Gentiles—they had become complacent or lost hope of making a significant impact. Perhaps they needed strong encouragement that God had prepared the way and that wherever faithful communities of his followers honor him with their lives and put his true character on display, people will notice and be drawn to him.

Although we don't know the specific message Paul brought to the community of God's people in Athens, his faithfulness to his God-given mission in such a powerful and dominant cultural environment can greatly encourage us as we seek to live out the mission in our broken culture. As people who believe that Jesus is Messiah, Savior, and Lord, we are called to imitate the way he lived and put God on display. As God's witnesses, we have been commissioned to bring the message by being the message. As we faithfully live out our calling, our Lord reigns, the "temple" of his people is built, and his kingdom is extended!

Yet the abundance of false gods and idols in our culture indicates that few people have known and experienced the true and living God we claim to serve.

> In what ways have we, as God's people who have been called to put him on display to the whole world, allowed the temples and idols of our culture to overshadow our portrayal of God's character and presence?

> What do you think Paul might "reason" with us about in regard to fulfilling our mission?

No matter how magnificent and influential the "temples" of our culture appear to be, God has prepared the way for his people to make him known. As God's temple, the visible representation of his kingdom in our world, perhaps it is time for us to examine our walk with God to see if we are portraying God and his kingdom faithfully.

In what ways do we diminish the influence of God's presence in our culture by:

- Being hypocritical or unfaithful?

- Living selfishly instead of imitating the way Jesus offered himself for the benefit of others?

- Behaving immorally or unethically, thus profaning God's character?

Study 3 | Clash of Kingdoms: God's Wisdom vs. the Wisdom of the Athenians

The Very Words of God

> *Where is the wise person? Where is the teacher of the law? Where is the*
> *philosopher of this age? Has not God made foolish the wisdom of the*
> *world? For since in the wisdom of God the world through its wisdom*
> *did not know him, God was pleased through the foolishness of what was*
> *preached to save those who believe.*

1 Corinthians 1:20–21

Bible Discovery

Paul Exposes the Myth of Human Wisdom

Paul came to Athens with a particular worldview and a mission to make it known. But the Hellenistic intellectuals of Athens—whether Stoic or Epicurean—were quite satisfied with their own worldview. Although they entertained discussion of new and different ideas, they already esteemed their own views and wisdom above all else. What would happen when Paul presented the truth of God's divine revelation to those who prided themselves on human wisdom?

When Paul spoke of his God, their thoughts went to their own gods represented by the beauty and perfection of Athens' many temples. When he spoke from the Scriptures, they were puzzled because their worldview was based on human logic and reason. Why would they need divine revelation? When he said that Jesus came to restore *shalom,* they wondered why they needed any peace other than the benefits *Pax Romana* had provided. When he shared the good news of the resurrection of Jesus, they would not even consider the possibility. Despite Paul's best efforts, it appears that not much "transformation" would take place in the minds of the Athenian elite. Their passion for the myth of their own wisdom made it difficult for them even to comprehend Paul's message.

So we wonder if Paul had the philosophers of Athens in mind
when he warned the Roman believers against being conformed
to the thinking patterns of the world, instructed them not to
think of themselves more highly than they ought, and encouraged them to be transformed by renewing their minds in accor-
dance with the mind of God.[14] Paul knew that human wisdom
was a myth made foolish by the wisdom of God. What could
he do to persuade the intellectuals of Athens that true wisdom
comes when our minds are transformed by the mind of God?

1. The Athenians were famous for their interest in philo-
    sophical and intellectual discussion. They never tired of
    talking about new ideas. One might say they were phi-
    losophy "junkies" in the way we describe people in our
    culture as information "junkies." What did Luke observe
    about the nature of their discussion? (See Acts 17:21.)

    Luke's observation of Athenian intellectual discussion was
    not exactly a compliment, but what opportunity did it
    provide for Paul, and how did he use it? (See Acts 17:17.)

DATA FILE
Why Did Paul Go to the Agora?

As in every other Roman city, the agora in Athens (or in Roman custom, *forum*) was the central gathering place for commercial, social, spiritual, and political activity. Typically, the agora was a large, open rectangular space around which were statues, monuments, altars, and temples. It functioned as the town marketplace offering permanent shops as well as temporary booths for farmers, merchants, and craftsmen to sell their goods. It also functioned as the official place of assembly where announcements were made on behalf of the Roman emperor as well as local authorities.

Often a covered colonnade, called a *stoa*, enclosed one or more sides of the agora. In Athens, the Stoics and Epicureans often gathered in one of the stoas of the agora to discuss and debate the latest ideas. In fact, the Stoics took their name from the fact that they could always be found in the *stoa*.

The reconstructed Stoa of Attalus pictured below was built on the eastern side of the agora in Athens. This two-story marble structure is 380 feet long and 65 feet wide. Each story had 21 rooms lit by doorways on the colonnade side and small windows on the back wall. The upper level had an Ionic colonnade and the lower a Doric. Stairways at each end of the stoa led to the second story.

The original structure was built between 159–138 BC by Attalos II, King of Pergamum. It was his gift of gratitude to the city of Athens for the education he had received there. Although the book of Acts does not tell us the exact location where Paul engaged the intellectuals and philosophers of Athens, the Stoa of Attalus was famous as one of their gathering places.

2. Everywhere he went in Greece, Paul presented the gospel
    message that Jesus the Messiah had come. He began by
    sharing his message in the Jewish synagogues, then went
    into the marketplace—the agora—to share the good news
    with anyone who would listen. In every city, the good
    news of God's kingdom captured the attention of influen-
    tial people—politicians, philosophers, religious leaders,
    business owners, and merchants. Without fail, Paul's radi-
    cal message hit a nerve that led to conflict and chaos.

    a. What was the nature of the uproar some Gentiles
        raised in response to Paul's message and actions in
        Philippi? (See Acts 16:16–24.)

    b. What about Paul's message upset both Jews and Gen-
        tiles in Thessalonica? (See Acts 17:1–8.)

    c. What key issue led to conflict in the Jewish synagogue
        in Corinth? (See Acts 18:12–17.)

  d. In what ways did the response to Paul's discussion
     and interaction with Gentiles in Athens differ from
     that in other cities? (See Acts 17:16–32.)

3. Paul made every effort to explain the good news of Jesus
   and his resurrection to anyone who would listen. Despite
   their self-proclaimed openness to discuss and debate Paul's
   ideas, how did the Athenian intellectuals actually respond
   to what he shared with them? (See Acts 17:18–20, 32.)

   What was the main point of Paul's message that they simply could not understand or accept? (See Acts 17:18, 32.)

   Although the Athenians expressed disdain for Paul and
   his message, what additional opportunity did they give
   him to explain himself? (See Acts 17:19–20.)

DATA FILE
Who Did Paul "Reason" with in the Agora?

In addition to would-be intellectuals who passed their time in the agora of Athens, there were educated philosophers known as the Stoics and Epicureans who prided themselves for having rational, logical, well-thought-out philosophies. The Stoics were the most influential, particularly among the ruling class including Emperor Nero. They belonged to the philosophical school founded by Zeno of Cyprus (340–265 BC).[15] The Epicureans, favored primarily by the upper classes, traced their philosophical system to Epicurus (341–270 BC).[16]

The Stoics took their name from the Stoa Poikile, a colonnade on the northern side of the agora where Zeno had taught. Their guiding life principle was using human reason to find harmony through rational knowledge of the natural law of the universe. They recognized a rational principle of order in all things and believed that the spark of the divine could be found in everything (pantheism). They believed fate controlled natural law and one's destiny, so they highly valued an attitude of harmony and calmness toward whatever fate decreed.

The Epicureans traced their philosophical views to 300 BC when Epicurus came to Athens, established a home, and spent the rest of his life teaching his views. Although he taught that the universe was the work of a creator deity, he believed that deity was no longer involved in the world and, therefore, was not relevant to daily life. Furthermore, he taught that humans are mortal and there is no life to come. For Epicureans, philosophical discussion was valued as the way of "salvation" that led to a fulfilling life. The goal of a good life was to enjoy whatever pleasure can be found while living modestly, gaining knowledge, and seeking freedom from pain, superstition, and anxiety.

4. In a letter to his disciple Timothy, Paul described people who would not accept truth or sound doctrine. In what ways is this a fitting description of the Athenians who Paul reasoned with in the agora? (See 2 Timothy 4:3–4.)

In what ways might this description apply to people we encounter in our world?

What can we, as God's people today, do to make God known in such situations?

Reflection

Culturally, intellectually, and spiritually Athens stood out among the greatest cities of the ancient world. No other city could boast of its philosophical heritage as the home of Aristotle, Plato, and Socrates. No other city could be home to the magnificent Parthenon, temple of Athena the patron goddess of Athens, set atop an expansive Acropolis three hundred feet above the city. No other city could match the beautiful array of temples found in Athens.

When Paul came to Athens, he naturally was impressed by what he saw. But he also recognized in Athens a culture built on the myth of Hellenism that elevated the human mind as the source of truth and wisdom. He saw a city of proud, self-satisfied intellectuals who did not know the true God. He saw them in constant pursuit of the myth of a logical, rational understanding of life, the myth that human reason could solve life's mysteries, and the myth that human ingenuity could bring *shalom* out of chaos.

In contrast, Paul understood that true wisdom is not based on the supremacy of the human mind but comes from a mind that is submitted to the mind of God and transformed by his revelation. Paul wanted more than anything to share the knowledge of the God he knew and the good news of Jesus with the people of Athens so that they could find *shalom*. So Paul explored Athens to see what people believed so that he could understand them and consider the best way to present the good news God had entrusted to him.

When Paul engaged the intellectuals of Athens, he was not afraid to listen, learn, and dialogue with them—even those with whom he passionately disagreed. As a rabbi, Paul likely would have been familiar with the belief of the Jewish sages that there is wisdom in understanding another person's perspective, especially when one disagrees with it. Luke's accounts of Paul's teaching give evidence that this was his pattern. He reasoned with them until they believed, rejected his ideas, or asked to hear more.

Our culture, like that of Athens, is built on the myth of Hellenism too. It is evident in our pursuit of wealth, leisure, and pleasure. It is evident in the assumption that the effort of the human mind—whether expressed in technology, education, or science—can correct the brokenness of our world and move us toward utopia. If we, followers of Jesus today, are intent on fulfilling the mission God has given to us, we need to take seriously Paul's example. By learning what others think and believe, we can better articulate our beliefs in a way that people who do not know God can understand.

How willing are we to understand and engage with—rather than ignore or shout at—those whose views differ from ours, especially if they reject a biblical worldview?

Do we consider it important enough to share the gospel with people who don't know God that we will read and listen to opinions of people with whom we disagree, or are we content to arrogantly ignore what is said or written by people whose opinions we dislike? Why?

How well do we know the worldview, beliefs, and lifestyle of our neighbors, including why they may disagree with our own?

In spite of the opposition Paul knew he would face, he was neither ashamed nor afraid to present the message of Jesus that God had entrusted to him. Even when people sneered, called him a babbler, and misrepresented his message, Paul persisted. His willingness to speak and live God's truth—whether it was popular, scorned, or led to great personal risk—is amazing.

How willing are we to be unpopular for making God known to others?

How willing are we to be mocked, rejected, or ignored in order to put God on display in the public square by what we say and how we live?

ENGAGING THE HEART: PAUL BEFORE THE AREOPAGUS

During the more than forty years I have taught the Bible in the locations where its stories unfolded, I have learned many inspiring insights into the meaning of the Text. On numerous occasions I have been deeply moved as I walked where Bible characters lived and experienced to some degree the geographic and cultural context where God made his presence known to them. One of those significant moments happened when I told the story of Paul's dramatic oration before the Areopagus, the religious court of ancient Athens, while standing within sight of where that event took place nearly two thousand years ago.

It was incredibly humbling to explain Paul's teaching near where he had taught it. It was inspiring to see some of what he saw as he taught and to understand more fully the power of his words that fit the context of that location so well. In his stirring speech to the Areopagus, using metaphors and images that came right out of the agora of Athens—the world center for philosophical debate and discussion—Paul displayed his extensive education and creative genius as he made known his "unknown" God.

As is often the case, I noticed things in the Text when I read it on site that I had not recognized before. For example, I had never realized that Paul likely presented his message within sight of the Parthenon, which was considered to be the most beautiful temple in the world. Paul was deeply committed to the mission of being God's witness—part of God's kingdom of priests being built up into his temple[1]—and making his presence known to all nations. So he explained to the idol-worshiping Athenians that God did not live in temples made with human hands. Imagine how powerful hearing that message would be. Imagine trying to understand the idea that Paul's God was too great to be contained in any temple—even the magnificent Parthenon that was so important to the people of Athens—and yet was near where people could find him. Paul was not merely telling his audience about God, he was using their surroundings to help them experience him!

For a long time, I had thought Paul was much like a Greek philosopher—biblically faithful, of course—in his approach to his mission. Like many Christians, I viewed him as presenting the good news by intellectual reasoning in the way the Greeks did. I thought he avoided presenting the good news through the testimony of the Text because the Greeks would not accept God's revelation. At the same time, I was uncomfortable with that assumption because I know the Text is God's inspired story. It provides knowledge about God, but more than that it shows how individual people came to know and experience a relationship with him. After I became more familiar with Hellenistic thinking and again read the account of Paul's presentation to the Areopagus, I realized that he had not avoided the Text at all. In fact, he had used it brilliantly to give his audience a picture of what God is like.

Of course, gaining a deeper understanding of how Paul carried out his ministry in Athens left me with questions too. I couldn't help but wonder why there is no mention in the Bible of a community of Jesus followers being established in Athens. Why didn't Paul's brilliant discourse touch the hearts of his audience? Why did so few respond? What is the key to making God near so that those who do not know will seek him and begin to experience who he is?

Opening Thoughts (3 minutes)

The Very Words of God

> *Then they took him and brought him to a meeting of the Areopagus,*
> *where they said to him, "May we know what this new teaching is that*
> *you are presenting? You are bringing some strange ideas to our ears,*
> *and we would like to know what they mean. . . ."*
>
> *Paul then stood up in the meeting of the Areopagus and said: "Peo-*
> *ple of Athens! I see that in every way you are very religious."*
>
> **Acts 17:19–20, 22**

Think About It

No matter what the topic, it seems that people who have differing perspectives often find it difficult to have a focused and
reasoned conversation about it. Haven't you witnessed or been
involved in discussions in which emotions or peripheral issues
became the central focus of the interaction and the core of the
matter was left unaddressed? It is disappointing to walk away
from such a discussion and realize that the most important issue
was never resolved or the key point was never mentioned. It is
tragic if that happens when the discussion is about the gospel
of Jesus. Yet often social issues, politics, or scientific controver-
sies become the focus of discussion (or disagreement) when we
attempt to have a conversation about Jesus.

What do you think is the key to keeping the focus on Jesus
and the good news of God's kingdom when we talk with
other people about our faith?

Video Notes (28 minutes)

Ancient temples built to bring the divine near

Paul connects with his audience through their worldview:
Introduces his God using their terminology

Explains his God through their ideas

Presents the big, new idea—the resurrection of Jesus

Paul connects with his audience using the Text:

Allusions to ideas and quotes from the Text

The Text achieves its purpose

You are God's Parthenon!

Video Discussion (8 minutes)

1. There was no better educated, more highly respected, or powerful audience in all of Athens than the Areopagus. This council represented the pinnacle of Athenian philosophy and politics, and it also functioned as the supreme court of Athens. Not only was the Areopagus the most coveted audience for presenting one's views, it was responsible for judging which views were permissible. In

the past, if a certain view was deemed unorthodox, the Areopagus had the power to impose the death penalty on its advocates. So Paul was given an amazing—and also dangerous—opportunity when he was invited to explain his God to the Areopagus.

a. In what ways did this audience differ from many of the people Paul spoke with when he visited other cities?

b. What do you think he hoped to accomplish by sharing the gospel of Jesus with the most powerful and influential people of Athens?

2. When Paul was called upon to explain the good news about his God to the political, religious, and cultural leaders of Athens, he likely did it with the Parthenon—that great symbol of Athens' identity, loyalty to their gods, and Hellenistic heritage—in view.

To better understand the layout and proximity of the key locations mentioned in Paul's story, study the map of Athens. Locate the Acropolis, a seven-and-a-half-acre rock outcropping that stood three hundred feet above the city, and its Parthenon. Locate the Areopagus (also called Mars Hill) on a lower hill. Then locate the agora below with its temples and stoas (where the Areopagus was also known to meet).

© Balage Balogh/www.ArchaeologyIllustrated.com

ATHENS DURING THE TIME OF PAUL: 1–PARTHENON, 2–ACROPOLIS, 3–AREOPAGUS (MARS HILL), 4–AGORA, 5–TEMPLE OF HEPHAESTUS

3. Imagine the challenge of sharing the identity and great-
    ness of the God of the Hebrews with the Acropolis and
    Parthenon towering in the background! How could Paul
    deliver his message and convince the Areopagus of God's
    greatness when God was "unknown" to them? How could
    he explain God's unfailing desire to restore his lost chil-
    dren to a relationship with him given what the Athenians
    believed about their gods? How could he translate the
    gospel message into the language of the Athenian culture?
    As it turned out, Paul did it brilliantly! Which of the ideas,
    words, and connection points familiar to the Athenians
    did Paul use to communicate who God is?

What did you notice about how effectively Paul used
what the Athenians knew to communicate with them?
How intriguing, for example, would news of an
"unknown God" be to this group of Greeks, and why?

If Paul were visiting our culture today, which key ideas,
words, and connection points do you think he might use
to capture the attention of and communicate with people
we know? *Fame, fortune, Power*

4. Paul was known as an exceptional student of one of the
most highly respected Jewish rabbis of his time. There
can be no doubt that he was thoroughly versed in the
Text and well-practiced in "reasoning" or vigorously dis-
cussing its meaning and application. What did you realize
about how much Paul used the Text in the context of
what the Athenians knew, in order to make God known
to them? *They loved to discuss new ideas.*

In light of the examples highlighted in the video of how Paul used the Text, such as the idea of God not living in a temple made by human hands, what are your thoughts about how we use the Bible to make God known in our world?

What do you think keeps us from using the Text more effectively when we share the good news of God with others?

5. Because of the Parthenon's unique structure, every stone in it was designed to fit in one place and one place only. In a similar way, God is uniquely shaping each of his followers to be a part of his temple—his Parthenon in a sense. How would you describe what it looks like for a follower of Jesus to stand out as God's temple, not as someone who shouts and judges but as someone who lives his or her life in a way that brings God near to those who don't know him? How well do you think we are doing this? *Become like Christ*

Small Group Bible Discovery and Discussion (16 minutes)

Paul Confronts the Truth of Idolatry

When Paul walked into Athens in 50 AD, he found a city unlike any he had visited previously. It was by no means the first pagan city Paul visited, but no other place rivaled the idolatry of Athens. There were more temples, altars, and idols in Athens than anywhere else in the ancient world. It truly was the idol capital of the Roman Empire. Even though the glorious golden age of classical Greece had faded into history, its legacy lived on in the superb quality of construction and artistry exhibited in the structures and statues that defined Athens.

But for Paul, the idolatry of Athens was heartbreaking. While others saw a magnificent and sophisticated city renowned as the religious, cultural, and philosophical heart of the ancient world, Paul saw an affront to the God who created heaven and earth. The entire city was dedicated to glorifying and worshiping every deity known in the Roman world! Everywhere Paul looked he saw praise, honor, and glory that was due to the God of the Hebrews and no other being given to every god imaginable.

Given that environment, what would happen when Paul shared the good news of God's kingdom in Athens? In the cities of Macedonia—Philippi, Thessalonica, Berea—Paul's message about Jesus and the kingdom of God was thought to undermine the power and authority of the Roman Empire and its deified emperor. The resulting economic and political conflict between the kingdom of this world and the news of the kingdom of God at times led to violent opposition and placed Paul in great danger. In Athens, Paul faced a different but also dangerous threat.

1. As a faithful Jew and student of the Text, Paul knew that idolatry—the praise and worship of gods people make for themselves—was an affront to God. When a human attributes power, accomplishments, and actions to deities other than God, it deprives him of the praise, glory, and honor that rightfully belong to him and no other. When Paul saw Zeus credited with creating the universe, or Athena praised for being the source of truth and wisdom, or Aesculapius honored as the one who heals, or the emperor hailed as the divine savior who brings peace, he was deeply grieved and offended. Zeus did not create. Athena is not the source of truth and wisdom. Aesculapius cannot heal. The emperor is not a divine giver of peace. As Paul understood the Text, God and God alone is all of these. Why would Paul believe that God alone is worthy of praise? (See 1 Chronicles 16:23–31; Psalm 96:1–9.)

2. Paul understood that the mission of God's people is to live in obedience, always bringing honor and praise to God through their words and actions so that other people may know—experience—who he is and come to praise him too. What does the Text reveal about how God wants to be known on earth, and how important is the honor and praise of his people in making him known? (See 1 Kings 8:56–60; 1 Chronicles 16:8–9; Psalm 46:10; 67:1–5.)

FOR GREATER UNDERSTANDING
What It Means to Know God

When people today say we *know* something, we usually think in terms of having a rational awareness or understanding *about* something. When we think of knowing God, for example, we tend to think in terms of knowing facts about him—his characteristics, what he does, what he says, how we should respond to him. Although it is good to know God in this way, such an understanding falls far short of the Hebrew concept of knowing God.

The Hebrew word usually translated as *know* in English is *yada. Yada* encompasses more than factual, rational knowledge. It is better understood as knowing or experiencing on a personal, or even intimate, level. Adam "knowing" Eve in the intimacy that resulted in the birth of a child would be an example of the personal and experiential connotation of *yada*.

God wants to be known, so when he called his people to the mission of living in such a way that the world would *know* him, he called them to far more than teaching a rational awareness or understanding of him. God called his people to be priests and witnesses who would not only proclaim but *be* his message to the world. He called his people to live as bearers of his image—living portraits, in a sense, of who and what God is. He has called all who follow him to demonstrate his character in every moment of life so that people who do not know him can experience (*yada*) who God is and give him the praise and honor he is due!

3. God protects his own identity and greatness. He declared, "I am the Lord; that is my name! I will not yield my glory to another or my praise to idols."[2] Therefore, God will not tolerate idolatry. He commands his people, those he has called as his partners in redemption, to give to him and no other the praise and honor he deserves.

a. What were God's specific commands and warnings to his people at Mount Sinai regarding idolatry, and how integral were those commands to the mission of making God known? (See Exodus 20:3–6; 34:10, 14–17.)

b. How vehemently does God hate idolatry, especially among the people he has called as his partners in redemption who are to demonstrate to the world that he is God? (See Deuteronomy 32:16–22; 2 Kings 17:15–20.)

4. In Paul's day, God's profound hatred of idolatry had become Israel's hatred too. Faithful Jews of Paul's time considered idolatry to be the ultimate sin, a violation of the very relationship they had with God and destructive to their calling as God's partners in redemption. So it is not surprising that Paul recognized idolatry as a great problem in Athens or that he was angered by the plethora of idols he found there. Always a man of action, Paul went first to the synagogue where both Jews and God-fearers knew the truth about idols. Then Paul went out into the agora—the public square as we would call it—and began making God known to those who obviously did not know him. (See Acts 17:17–20.)

a. By speaking with the Stoics and Epicureans in the agora of Athens, Paul was engaging the most educated Gentiles in the Greco-Roman world. How did they respond to the good news of Jesus that Paul taught?

b. Which idea(s) of Paul's particularly concerned them, and what was their solution?

DID YOU KNOW?
What Was the Areopagus?

Just below the sacred entrance to the Acropolis of Athens is a smaller limestone hill topped by a large, mostly flat mass of rock known as the "rock of Ares" (Ares is the Greek god of war) or *Areopagus*. After Athens became part of the Roman Empire, the hill also was known as Mars Hill (Mars being the Roman god of war). But the term *Areopagus* also referred to the judicial body that took its name from the hill and was known as the "Council of the Areopagus" or simply, "Areopagus." So the term could refer to the hilltop location or to the council.

Originally the council likely met on the hill from which it took its name, but by Paul's time the council met somewhere in the Royal Stoa of the agora located at the foot of the hill. The Areopagus council originally was the governing body of Athens, but as democracy evolved it assumed more of a judicial function. The council had jurisdiction over serious crimes, including murder, and was the designated guardian of religious orthodoxy. By Paul's time, it was responsible for maintaining order in the city and the piety of religious practice.

In Luke's account of Paul's appearance before the Areopagus, it seems clear that the term applies to the council, not the hill. Paul stands "in the midst of" a group of people rather than a location (Acts 17:22). One of the two people who believed Paul's message is described as being a member of the Areopagus (Acts 17:34), which certainly means the council. The group Paul addressed was not small. The council comprised about a hundred lifelong members who held high public office, and a number of philosophers and interested observers were likely present to hear what Paul had to say.

5. The Areopagus had long been a powerful influence in Athens. Its responsibilities included maintaining order and ensuring the piety of religious practice by preventing heresy and the worship of new deities. Given the fact that some of his listeners in the agora thought Paul was advocating foreign gods and teaching strange ideas—charges similar to what the Areopagus had sentenced Socrates to death for centuries earlier—how serious a situation does it seem Paul faced? (See Acts 17:18–20.)

Serious

According to the words of Jesus, how prepared was Paul to address the charges against him by explaining the good news of God's kingdom? (See Matthew 10:17–20.)

DID YOU KNOW?
They "Brought" Paul to a Meeting of the Areopagus

Every time Paul proclaimed the message of God's kingdom that Jesus is Messiah, Savior, and Lord, conflict with the kingdom of this world followed. This was true in the cities of Macedonia—Philippi, Thessalonica, Berea—and it would be true in the cities of Achaia—Athens and Corinth—as well. In Athens, the trouble started when Paul began reasoning with philosophers in the agora.

As "open" to new ideas as the intellectuals of Athens thought themselves to be, they didn't exactly accept what Paul shared with them. They called him names and suspected him of "advocating foreign gods." Then they brought him to a meeting of the Areopagus and asked him to explain himself.

From our perspective two thousand years later, it is easy to think the invitation for Paul to address the Areopagus was a great opportunity to present God's story to the intellectual elite of the Roman Empire. And it was, but it was also complicated. Luke's word choices in his record of the event[3]—translated as "they took" and "brought" him to the Areopagus—suggest that this was more than a friendly invitation. Luke's Greek words convey the nuance of taking someone by force and are the same words used when an angry crowd "brought" Paul before the proconsul in Corinth.[4] So it appears that Paul's invitation to appear before the Areopagus was not an elective visit to a friendly philosophy discussion group.

The opportunity for Paul to present his "philosophy of Jesus" to the Areopagus carried significant risk. The council was responsible to examine any new teaching to ensure it did not violate any of the existing gods and rituals and to verify the ancient history of the proposed god. If the council approved the legitimacy of the teaching, the deity could be added to the plethora of gods already worshiped as long as its advocates provided funding for a temple, priesthood, and accompanying ritual. If the Areopagus rejected the deity, those advocating the new god would be punished. In fact, in the past the punishment for introducing unknown gods was severe. Four centuries before Paul walked into Athens the Areopagus had sentenced Socrates, the famous Greek philosopher, to death for similar charges!

Paul knew his audience would not be persuaded easily. Unlike many of his audiences, they did not know the Scriptures. Furthermore, they had their philosophy figured out and had little, if any, interest in change. Paul, however, was "not ashamed of the gospel."[5] Fearlessly he proclaimed his message that challenged not only their religious practices but their whole life paradigm.

He turned the official practice upside down, revealing that they would not be judging God. Rather, the Creator God who was formerly "unknown" to them sat in judgment of them! The God Paul proclaimed did not live in temples, was not represented by images made with hands, nor was he served by human hands as if he needed anything. In fact, the God Paul proclaimed provided all of these things for the entire human race! So Paul left his Areopagus audience pondering the clear message: Humans do not get to define who God, their Creator, is and God has proclaimed Jesus as Messiah and Lord.

Faith Lesson (4 minutes)

Although we don't have statues, altars, and temples for named deities scattered throughout our cities, our culture is, neverthe-less, idolatrous. Paul shared the gospel message in many cities where idol worship was the predominant practice, so by observing his experience we can learn how to better fulfill the mission Jesus has given to everyone who follows him. Paul's approach and method for sharing the gospel in the idol-worshiping cities of Athens, Ephesus, and Lystra is most instructive:

- We have explored how Paul "reasoned" with Stoics, Epicure-ans, and anyone else who would listen in Athens. He used every available opportunity to explain the gospel in the con-text, images, and language Athenians would understand.

- Regarding Paul's time in Ephesus, the world center for Arte-mis worship, we have no record of specific speeches Paul gave to Gentile idol worshipers there. We do know what others said about his teaching, and their testimony says he was never critical or insulting of Artemis or her worshipers.[6]

- In Lystra, Paul healed a lame man. When people saw this, they went wild thinking that Paul (as well as his compan-ion, Barnabas) was one of their own gods visiting them in human form. The people were ready to offer sacrifices to

Paul when he stopped them and told them the good news about the living God.[7]

In each of these cities, Paul taught that gods made by human hands are not gods at all. He made every effort to build bridges of understanding with his audience so that he could connect his message with what they knew, what they believed, and how they lived. He had no need to judge, criticize, disparage, or condemn their beliefs but instead presented the truth of God's message, allowing his audience to consider its implications and their response.

Paul's approach to sharing the gospel in these cities is evangelistic, yes, but it is pastoral as well. His evangelistic concern is evident in his careful explanation of God's story using biblical concepts in a way his audience would understand. He was not asking for rational agreement or even to engage in argument but desired a response of faith. His presentation is pastoral in his concern for his audience to experience the living God. His teaching bears no hostility, anger, or condemnation. Instead, he emphasizes God's compassion, mercy, and patience.

THINK ABOUT IT
Paul's Message to Worshipers of Idols: Pastoral and Evangelistic

Paul Presents the Essential Elements of the Gospel	In Lystra	In Athens
There is one living God	Acts 14:15	Acts 17:24
God is the Creator of all	Acts 14:15	Acts 17:24
God is the provider of all	Acts 14:17	Acts 17:25
God is kind, patient, and caring for all of his children, even if they do not know him	Acts 14:17	Acts 17:27–28
In the past, God tolerated the ignorance and idolatry of those who did not know him	Acts 14:16	Acts 17:23, 30
God makes himself known: in Lystra by agricultural abundance, in Athens as the god they call the unknown god	Acts 14:17	Acts 17:23
God wants everyone to repent and turn to him	Acts 14:15	Acts 17:30–31

Unfortunately, we often are not at all like Paul—or Jesus—when we present our faith to those who do not know God. It is tempting to follow the ways of our negative, confrontational culture and be judgmental, critical, rude, and demeaning rather than expressing pastoral compassion and patience. We often find it easier to criticize and condemn than to engage in personal interaction that may lead to a life-changing experience with God. We may be comfortable sharing what we believe but not evangelistic enough to face possible rejection or mockery when we invite a commitment to God's way of thinking.

1. Even with the most pagan Gentiles, Paul built bridges of communication and understanding in a caring, pastoral way. What must you do differently in order to be more pastoral in your efforts to make God known in your world?

   • In your attitude?

   Be like Christ

   • In your approach?

   • In your words?

2. Paul was a master at leading an audience through God's story and then fearlessly inviting them to join that story. What might you do differently in order to be more evangelistic in your efforts to make God known in your world?

What will you do in order to know the Text well enough to explain it to someone who is not already familiar with it?

How willing are you to "eat with sinners" and respect them enough to learn about their beliefs so that you are able to address their perspective effectively?

How deep is your love for people who do not yet know God, and what are you willing to sacrifice in order to present God's call to faith and obedience?

Closing (1 minute)

Read Acts 17:24–27, 30 aloud together: "The God who made the world and everything in it is the Lord of heaven and earth and does not live in temples built by human hands. And he is not served by human hands, as if he needed anything. Rather, he himself gives everyone life and breath and everything else. From one man he made all the nations, that they should inhabit the whole earth; and he marked out their appointed times in history and the boundaries of their lands. God did this so that they would seek him and perhaps reach out for him and find him, though he is not far from any one of us . . . now he commands all people everywhere to repent."

Then pray, thanking God that he has made himself known to you. Praise him that he—and he alone—is Creator, Savior, God, and King. Thank him for the privilege of choosing you to serve as his partner in redemption. With a grateful heart for the way he has prepared the way, ask him to guide you in preparing yourself to share the gospel message and in remaining alert to opportunities to make him known. Restate to him your commitment to carry his presence into the world you live in so that those who are lost in their empty pursuit of false gods may come to know and worship him as Savior and Lord too.

Memorize

> *The God who made the world and everything in it is the Lord of heaven and earth and does not live in temples built by human hands. And he is not served by human hands, as if he needed anything. Rather, he himself gives everyone life and breath and everything else. From one man he made all the nations, that they should inhabit the whole earth; and he marked out their appointed times in history and the boundaries of their lands. God did this so that they would seek him and perhaps reach out for him and find him, though he is not far from any one of us . . . now he commands all people everywhere to repent.*

Acts 17:24–27, 30

Making God Known in a Broken World

In-Depth Personal Study Sessions

Study 1 | Paul Spoke the Language of the Culture

The Very Words of God

> *The God who made the world and everything in it is the Lord of heaven and earth and does not live in temples built by human hands. And he is not served by human hands, as if he needed anything. Rather, he himself gives everyone life and breath and everything else.*

Acts 17:24–25

Bible Discovery

"I See You Are Very Religious . . ."

Paul was deeply schooled in the Text and filled with God's Spirit. Even so, proclaiming the good news of God's kingdom in Athens was a challenge. If he spoke of God, his audience would likely wonder, *Which one?* If he explained how to be saved, they likely would wonder, *From what?* If he mentioned the requirements of the Law, they might wonder, *The law?* If Paul spoke to them using such terminology they would have no idea what he was talking about. Their confusion would only increase if he spoke of sin, the prophets, Messiah, or a kingdom that is not of this world. They not only didn't know the language of the gospel, they had no understanding of its concepts.

Paul, of course, was no ordinary teacher, and he was determined to reach his audience. So he went to the synagogue, engaging Jews and God-fearers in discussion and debate. He also discussed the good news with philosophers he encountered in the agora. Some were puzzled by his message. Others recognized its radical implications and invited him to the Areopagus, their supreme religious council, to more thoroughly explain the God he was talking about.

Through this invitation, God had opened a rare opportunity for Paul to share his faith with an influential audience. True to his mission and character, Paul approached the opportunity with everything he had. Although time was short, he prepared for his presentation to the Areopagus by looking "carefully" at the Athenians' objects of worship in order to become familiar with their beliefs and practices. He then spoke brilliantly, presenting the Text in the context of their world and even using rhetorical devices of their own great orators.

But Paul did not leave the philosophers and skeptics of Athens with intriguing ideas to discuss endlessly. He explained God's story with passion and concluded with proof that gave no alternative but to join the story or to reject it. Let's see what we can learn from Paul that will help us engage the self-satisfied, skeptical people of our own broken culture with the good news about Jesus.

1. Paul's greatest opportunity to share the gospel message in Athens came when the Areopagus asked him to explain himself regarding the charge that he was advocating the worship of foreign deities. Responsible to protect the order and orthodoxy of the city, the Areopagus had the authority not only to pass judgment on the matter but to authorize punishment for infractions. So it was vitally important for Paul to present the message of God's great story in an engaging and informative manner the Athenians would understand. Let's consider what Paul had to keep in mind as he prepared himself for the challenge.

   a. Paul needed to communicate God's story of redemption that began millennia before his day in the lives of Abraham and Sarah and the Hebrews at Mount Sinai. Jews loved the ancient stories that demonstrated

God's faithfulness over time, and they valued new ideas that extended or completed God's ancient revelation. In contrast, what captured the interest of the people of Athens? (See Acts 17:21.)

The immediate

How do you think Paul could present his message in a way that stimulated their curiosity?

How might it be possible to deliver a message that is both ancient in its roots and radically new at the same time?

b. Paul needed to find what we call "points of contact" between his own perspective and that of his audience so that what he said would be relevant to their daily experience. As he explored the city, what discovery gave Paul a connection point to frame his defense against the charge of advocating unknown gods and the message of the gospel? (See Acts 17:23.)

The Unknown God

How did this discovery aid his defense?

What opportunity did it give him to share the good news of Jesus?

THINK ABOUT IT
Paul Found an Altar to an "Unknown" God

Luke's account of Paul's visit to Athens mentions Paul finding an altar inscribed "TO AN UNKNOWN GOD."[8] This altar, which members of the Areopagus knew about as well, provided an essential connection point that allowed Paul to share the good news of God's story in his presentation to them. In addition to mention of the altar in the book of Acts, several ancient writers refer to such altars,[9] but none has been found in Athens.

Not having found the altar "to the unknown god" in Athens, we don't know what it looked like. However, another altar (pictured below) dedicated to the "unknown god" has been found in the outer court of the temple of Demeter in Pergamum.

We also do not know the purpose or function of this altar in Athens. We don't know if it was placed to honor the "unknown" god just to be safe in case they were offending it. Or if it was an altar to the God of the Jews who the Athenians labeled as "unknown" because the Jews didn't speak his name or make images of him.[10] Or if the altar simply did not have a name on it so the god it honored was presumed "unknown."[11]

In addition, there is an ancient Athenian myth to consider. According to the story, there was a severe plague for which the priests had sacrificed to every known god to no avail. A wise man named Epimenides advised the priests to let a flock of sacrificial sheep wander around and then, wherever the sheep rested, to build an altar and make sacrifices to the "unknown god" who they assumed was responsible for the plague.[12]

Regardless of the altar's original purpose, it fit perfectly into God's plan for Paul to present the gospel to the most educated and influential leaders of Athens.

  c. Paul also needed to find a way to connect with (as well as critique) the predominant philosophies of the Epicureans and Stoics. He began by addressing the common ground of both schools of thought, which focused on the role of temples. The Epicureans taught that temples were unnecessary because the gods were uninvolved in the matters of daily human life. The Stoics believed that temples were unnecessary because God was already present in everything—including temples. How interested do you think they were and what might they have thought when Paul said that God "does not live in temples built by human hands" (Acts 17:24)?

      In what ways did Paul's statement about God's presence and care for his children (see Acts 17:27–28)

refute the Epicurean perspective that deities were
largely absent from involvement in daily life? Why
would this matter?

The Stoics were pantheists, believing that everything
contains the divine presence and that the divine
presence is in everything. What clear distinctions did
Paul make between God and his creation that would
challenge the Stoic view? (See Acts 17:24–27, 31.)

2. The oratorical style and customary elements of presen-
    tation before the Areopagus were well established. So
    Paul adopted the techniques of a Greek orator in order
    to plead his case. Even his opening greeting and style of
    "reasoning" fit the practice of the Areopagus.

    a. Speeches typically began by praising the audience,
        in this case, the "people of Athens." (See Acts 17:22.)
        What did Paul tell the Athenians he had noticed about
        them, and how do you think these people who prided
        themselves in their many gods, temples, statues, and
        altars felt about his comment?

        Religious

b.   Greek intellectuals engaged in discussion and debate
     by reasoning (*dialegomai*, in Greek). A "reasoned"
     presentation would include the use of precedent, the
     defense of one's own position, the critique of other
     positions, and the use of philosophical sources to
     build the foundation for a conclusion. Socrates used
     this method with his philosophical opponents, taking
     the opposite side of an issue and discussing it un-
     til a synthesis based on human reason was reached.
     The Jews used a similar discussion style in which the
     speaker's point of view was presented and supported
     by various interpretations of the Hebrew Bible (in
     contrast to the Greek dependence on human reason).
     What was the subject of Paul's "reasoned" presenta-
     tion? (See Acts 17:23.)

PERSONAL PROFILE
Paul, Prepared to Address the Areopagus

Paul was uniquely qualified to present the gospel message to the Gentile
world. He was born in Tarsus in Cilicia, a commercial hub known for its great
wealth and a university equal to those in Athens and Alexandria. Brought up
in Jerusalem as the son of a faithful Jewish family, he likely received an
excellent education in the Torah. Later, Paul studied under Gamaliel, one
of the most highly respected Torah experts and a great Jewish sage who
taught his disciples about the Greek and Roman worldview so that they
could apply the Torah to life in their world.

To be a student of Gamaliel, Paul must have been brilliant (and inspired) in
his knowledge and interpretation of the Hebrew Text. Gamaliel, whose interpretations of the Text were often similar to those of Jesus, clearly influenced
Paul's teaching. In addition, he taught Greek Wisdom so that his disciples
could apply the Torah to the Hellenistic worldview of Imperial Rome.

Using this background, Paul explored Athens in order to learn all he could about his audience. He knew the importance of identifying points of contact that would enable him to present the gospel in a way idol-worshiping Athenians would readily understand. His presentation of the good news to the Areopagus demonstrated the brilliant way Jewish rabbis can explain the meaning of the Text using the metaphors and word pictures of their audience.

Like Moses, Paul had an unusual background of training and experience that prepared him for exactly the task God intended. As they were growing up, Moses and Paul could not have known how God would use them in his plan, yet each was prepared for his task in every way.[13]

3. Paul's reasoned presentation about the "unknown" God gave him a brilliant defense against the charge that he was introducing a new and foreign deity. The Athenians already recognized the God Paul wanted to tell them about! In what ways did the ability to talk about the "unknown" God open the door for Paul to tell the Areopagus anything he wanted to say about the God he loved and knew so well? (See Acts 17:23.)

What was Paul able to explain about: (See Acts 17:23–31.)
• Who God is

• What God does

- What God cares about

- Who we are in relationship to God

- What God wants from us

- Why it is important for us to respond to him

How complete a summary of the gospel message did Paul present to the Areopagus?

Reflection

Paul's opening statement to the Areopagus (Acts 17:22–23) is instructive for anyone who has an opportunity to share God's story with people who do not know him, especially if they aren't particularly interested in knowing him. Paul's respectful and complimentary, "I see that in every way you are very religious," bears no hint of accusation or criticism. Rather, it is engaging and positive, opening the ears and minds of his listeners for what follows: "this is what I am going to proclaim to you."

Although his audience would not know it until he finished, Paul would give them far more than an inspiring speech. In that most pagan city, he planned to carry out the calling God gave to his people at Mount Sinai. He wanted his audience to know and experience who God is. His goal was to invite his audience to join God's story and become followers of Jesus. So he was not about to let his attitude or actions become a barrier to that goal.

As followers of Jesus today, we have a lot to learn from Paul's approach. Far too often we are negative and critical when we engage those who do not share our faith or lifestyle. In our efforts to make God's truth known, which of course we cannot compromise, we sometimes judge, label, and condemn the very people we want to reach. By doing so we close people's minds and hearts. Because of our lack of interest, respect, and concern for them, they resist the message and example that God has entrusted to us to share with the world.

If we want to bring and be God's message to people who do not know him, we must begin seeing them as God sees them. We must be committed to the truth that God wants all of his lost children to come to him and experience who he is. Toward this end, Paul invested time and energy into getting to know the people of Athens. He entered their world in order to understand what they believed and why. He studied their beliefs and practices so that his words and example would communicate clearly. He did everything he could to earn the right to engage them in meaningful dialogue. He then was able to present God's story in a way that engaged their beliefs and assured them that they mattered to Paul and to the God he represented.

Paul walked into the "foreign" culture of Athens and continued walking and observing until he could conclude, "I see that you are very religious."

What might Paul observe about our culture?

How might he complete this sentence about our culture: "I
see you are very *selfish*

How might we complete the sentence, "I see you are very
_____ " if we were to study our own culture from the perspective of wanting to understand it rather than judging it?

Obviously Paul, a faithful Jew and follower of Jesus, faced significant challenges in his effort to present the gospel in the cultural
"language" of Athens.

What do you think would be Paul's greatest challenge in presenting the gospel in the "language" of our culture? Why?

In what ways might speaking to our culture be more difficult
or easier than what he faced in Athens?

What might Paul do or say differently from what we typically
do or say when we present the gospel?

What specific things might we do to better understand our culture, and in what ways might we speak to it more effectively?

Study 2 | Paul Knew the Text

The Very Words of God

> *As the rain and the snow come down from heaven, and do not return to it without watering the earth and making it bud and flourish, so that it yields seed for the sower and bread for the eater, so is my word that goes out from my mouth: It will not return to me empty, but will accomplish what I desire and achieve the purpose for which I sent it.*
>
> *Isaiah 55:10–11*

Bible Discovery

Paul Speaks to the Culture from the Text

Paul began his presentation to the Areopagus with his observation that they were very religious. He then proceeded to tell them about his God—the one they didn't know—through the cultural norms and metaphors of life as they understood and lived them. But Paul wasn't standing before the Areopagus simply to have a lively discussion about Athenian culture. He was there to share a life-changing message that would shake that culture to its foundation. While he clearly and brilliantly presented his message in the "language" of the culture, his message came straight out of the Hebrew Bible!

Although they were too ignorant of the Bible to realize it, Paul gave the philosophers of Athens a Bible study! Paul shared a concise summary of God's redemptive story using words, phrases, and allusions straight out of the Hebrew Text. As brilliant a student, skilled a teacher, and gifted a communicator as Paul was, he did not depend on his own skill and human wisdom to make his case to the Areopagus. Fulfilling his mission was too important to risk that. Instead, Paul took the promise of Isaiah 55:10–11 to heart and spoke to his audience from God's Word:

> As the rain and the snow come down from heaven, and do not return to it without watering the earth and making it bud and flourish, so that it yields seed for the sower and bread for the eater, so is my word that goes out from my mouth: It will not return to me empty, but will accomplish what I desire and achieve the purpose for which I sent it.

Certainly human words can be blessed and have a powerful effect, but God's Word *always* accomplishes God's intended purpose. By using God's Word as the basis for his message, Paul was in effect claiming the promise that God would anoint those words to have the effect he desired. With that intent, Paul boldly shared the good news of Jesus through a carefully reasoned presentation from the Scriptures.

1. Within a few moments, any Jews or God-fearers in Paul's audience would have known the source of Paul's message. His words echoed familiar portions of the sacred scrolls they had heard read many times in their synagogue. Most Jesus followers today, however, are far less familiar with God's Word. So take a fresh look at Paul's speech before the Areopagus and consider the textual background of his major points. In the chart of Paul's presentation below, connect each of the points (A–G) Paul makes to the corresponding source passage(s) in the Hebrew Text. You may have more than one point for a particular passage.

Background Hebrew Text	A–G?	Paul's Teaching—Acts 17:24–31
Genesis 1:1–2:7		A The God who made the world and everything in it is the Lord of heaven and earth and does not live in temples built by human hands.
Genesis 9:1, 18–19		
Deuteronomy 4:27–31		
Deuteronomy 10:14		B And he is not served by human hands, as if he needed anything. Rather, he himself gives everyone life and breath and everything else.
Deuteronomy 32:8		
1 Kings 8:27		
2 Chronicles 6:18		C From one man he made all the nations, that they should inhabit the whole earth; and he marked out their appointed times in history and the boundaries of their lands.
Psalm 50:9–12		
Psalm 96:13		D God did this so that they would seek him and perhaps reach out for him and find him, though he is not far from any one of us.
Psalm 100:3		
Psalm 115:2–9, 14–15		E "For in him we live and move and have our being." As some of your own poets have said, "We are his offspring."
Isaiah 42:5		
Isaiah 44:9–10, 21–22		F Therefore since we are God's offspring, we should not think that the divine being is like gold or silver or stone—an image made by human design and skill.
Isaiah 46:5–10		
Isaiah 55:6		
Jeremiah 10:11–12		G In the past God overlooked such ignorance, but now he commands all people everywhere to repent. For he has set a day when he will judge the world with justice by the man he has appointed.
Jeremiah 29:13		
Malachi 2:15		

Paul clearly structured his argument on the Text. In what ways is what he did different from the way we often build a case for the gospel message?

What might we learn from Paul's example about how to focus on presenting the message of God's Word in a culturally aware context?

How confident are we of the sufficiency of God's Word to accomplish what God desires as we seek to make him known, and why?

DID YOU KNOW?
God Does Not Live in Temples Made by Human Hands

As a young Pharisee, Paul vigorously defended the Hebrew Scriptures and the traditions of the Jewish faith. He was a witness to Stephen's defense to the Sanhedrin against charges of blasphemy that arose from Stephen's testimony of Jesus. The offense was related to rumors of Jesus' statement about the destruction of the temple in Jerusalem and potentially threatening changes to the Jewish understanding of the traditions Moses established.

Stephen's defense of the gospel was a powerful testimony of God's redemption story—a story Paul knew well from his own study of the Text. However, Stephen's statements that "the Most High does not live in houses made by human hands,"[14] his accusations of the Jewish leaders' refusal to believe, and his vision of the Son of Man (Jesus) at the right hand of God was too much for his audience. They stoned him and Paul approved. Yet, after Paul came to faith in Jesus as his Messiah, he spent the rest of his life proclaiming the same truth Stephen had proclaimed. He even used the same words as Stephen to testify before the council of idol worshipers in Athens. Did he remember that moment as he spoke to the Areopagus?

2. The most striking point of Paul's message, where he speaks directly and powerfully to the cultural environment in Athens, is in Acts 17:24: "The God who made the world and everything in it is the Lord of heaven and earth and does not live in temples built by human hands." Imagine Paul standing outside near the Acropolis or in the stoa and explaining that the God he wanted them to know—their "unknown" god—didn't live in temples made by hands!

   Regardless of the precise meeting location of the Areopagus, they were surrounded by temples of all kinds—each one made by human hands! Imagine Paul looking around at the amazing array of temples, statues, and shrines for which Athens was renowned as he made this statement. Or, imagine him gesturing toward the beautiful Parthenon above them to draw attention to their proudly held Greek ideals as their orators often did. Why would this comment have been so provocative in that environment, and what questions do you think it raised in the minds of his audience?

THINK ABOUT IT
A God Too Great for the Parthenon!

Try to imagine the irony of Paul standing in sight of the most impressive and beautiful temple known in the world and declaring that his God, the maker of heaven and earth, did not live in temples made by human hands. No doubt it was nearly impossible for the Athenian elite to comprehend a god that was too great to be confined to any temple, especially one of theirs. After all, the Greeks sought absolute perfection in building the exquisite sculptures and magnificent temples that made Athens a showcase for Greek superiority. Even their conquerors, the Romans, celebrated the genius of the Greek masterpieces and displayed significant numbers of them in Rome to enhance their own culture.

The Parthenon, built on the fortress-like Acropolis that towered three hundred feet above the lower city of Athens, was the most iconic temple of all. Built entirely of marble, its grace and beauty was unsurpassed. Covering an area about half the size of a football field, its forty-six outer columns stood about thirty-five feet tall and supported a roof tiled with marble. Situated on the Acropolis, the Parthenon epitomized the golden era of Greek civilization in the fifth century BC. Even today it is renowned as one of the most recognizable sites in the world.

Built for Athena, the goddess of wisdom, the Parthenon was the ultimate visual statement of the wisdom and knowledge the Greeks believed their gods had entrusted to them. It displayed what the Greeks prized most: order, beauty, harmony, rationality, human accomplishment, and perfection. Despite all that, the Parthenon was unworthy and insufficient to contain the God Paul proclaimed! Paul used the visible example of the Parthenon to illustrate that the God he proclaimed was the Creator and provider of everything and that even the best efforts of his creation could not make a space appropriate for him. And Paul expressed this by using a statement straight from God's own story!

Reflection

As a young Pharisee, Paul loved God and was committed to obey all of his commands and to defend the Jewish faith against all threats. Like many other faithful Jews, he was convinced that followers of Jesus, perhaps because of their acceptance of Gentiles into their fellowship, violated the Scriptures. For this offense, he believed zealous violence against them was fully justified. That is why he actively persecuted Christians before he met Jesus on the road to Damascus.

Paul was present when a follower of Jesus named Stephen was arrested and required to defend himself to the Jewish religious council regarding his alleged statements about the Lord's temple in Jerusalem. Stephen proceeded to give an impassioned defense of God's redemptive story, filling his speech with references to and quotes from the Hebrew Text.

When Stephen reached the part of the story where Solomon dedicated the temple of the Lord, he echoed a portion of Solomon's prayer, "But will God really dwell on earth with humans? The heavens, even the highest heavens, cannot contain you. How much less this temple I have built!"[15] He also quoted the prophet Isaiah who, standing in the very temple Solomon had built, spoke these words from God: "Heaven is my throne and the earth is my footstool. Where is the house you will build for me? Where will my resting place be? Has not my hand made all these things, and so they came into being?"[16] Stephen then concluded, "the Most High does not live in houses made by human hands."[17]

As Stephen continued his defense, proclaiming Jesus as the Son of God, his audience became infuriated. While Paul watched and approved of it all, they stoned Stephen to death. But not long thereafter, Paul met Jesus who led him to repentance and a life wholly committed to declaring the same truth from the same Text that Stephen proclaimed.

As Paul matured in his faith, he surely was deeply grieved by how little he had understood the Text when Stephen proclaimed it. But the words of God, spoken faithfully by Stephen, were burned into Paul's mind and soul. When it came time for him to defend himself to the Areopagus in Athens, Paul used some of the very words of Scripture Stephen had used to make God known to the council of idol worshipers in Athens.

God's Word is the very foundation of who we are. When it goes out into the world, it always achieves the purpose for which God intends. While it is true that we need to know and engage the culture effectively, we must engage it as men and women who speak the truth of the Text.

God is always looking for people who address the culture through the Text. What is your commitment to be one of them?

What is your commitment to learning the Text so that it will become a part of your life and witness?

Study 3 | You Are God's Parthenon

The Very Words of God

When they heard about the resurrection of the dead, some of them sneered, but others said, "We want to hear you again on this subject." At that, Paul left the Council. Some of the people became followers of Paul and believed. Among them was Dionysius, a member of the Areopagus, also a woman named Damaris, and a number of others.

Acts 17:32–34

Bible Discovery

A Lukewarm Reception for Paul's Powerful Proclamation

The philosophers of Athens spent their days contentedly talking about whatever new idea caught their interest. Paul, however, had a mission. His purpose and goal was to make God known so that all people would know and experience him and give him the honor and praise that he alone deserved. Paul's desire for the people of Athens was the same as for anyone else he encountered: to leave their idols behind and join the story of the one true God.

Paul's proclamation before the Areopagus is brilliant. He delivered it according to Greek oratorical practice, connecting with his audience through familiar images and metaphors of life in Athens and providing carefully chosen content that critiqued their philosophical perspective. He established a Scripture-based foundation for God's identity and built it to completion with allusions and quotes from the Text.

Paul first proclaimed that the God "unknown" to them was none other than the Creator and sustainer of the universe. Then he established God as the provider on whom all life depends and who needs nothing from his created offspring. Finally, he presented history as God's story, identifying God as the one who controls and acts in all of history. History, then, is not cyclical (as the Greeks believed) but is moving toward a grand climax. Paul assembled his proclamation in such a way that it demanded a response of belief and action, concluding with a call to repentance and acceptance of God's story.

We can almost feel the unease in the council growing as Paul built his powerful case for God. But what impact would Paul's presentation have? How would his audience respond? Would they believe and act on what he said or walk away and wait for the next new idea to come along? As much as Paul wanted to make God known, it is interesting that he didn't seek to prove or argue for his perspective. He knew that those who rejected his proclamation would also reject his conclusions. His mission was to proclaim the message, to make God's Word known, and to allow God's Spirit to do the persuading and accomplish God's purpose.

1. Paul's brilliant proclamation of God's great story of redemption was powerful, concise, profound, and culturally relevant. Even those who did not agree with him likely appreciated his presentation and discussed and debated it for years. Although his Greek audience would have been proud to receive affirmation and praise for such a genius performance, Paul wanted something entirely different.

    a. Where did Paul want the glory for his presentation to be directed, and why? (See 1 Chronicles 16:8; Isaiah 12:4.)

    b. Although Hellenists would seek praise from their audience, what kind of response did Paul want from his audience? (See Acts 17:30; James 2:17.)

    Aceptance
    Redemption

> ## FOR GREATER UNDERSTANDING
> ### What Does It Mean to Repent?
> In the metaphorical language of the Hebrews, God calls his people to walk on his path, the path of righteousness.[18] People who are disobedient are said to have left the right path and chosen the evil path.[19] To "repent" (Hebrew, *tshuva*) literally means to "return" or change one's path to the right path.
>
> Repentance is more than simply acknowledging that one is on the wrong path or accepting that God's way is the right path. To repent is to return to God's path of righteousness. So, when Paul tells the Areopagus that God "commands all people to repent," he is asking them to:
>
> • Acknowledge that their Greek way is not God's way,
>
> • Reject Hellenism and idolatry,
>
> • Change their walk and become God-fearers who walk on God's path.

2. The Jewish understanding of God in relationship to the idolatry of pagan nations was traditionally one of patience and mercy rather than judgment and punishment. Moses wrote, "The LORD is slow to anger, abounding in love and forgiving sin and rebellion."[20] Jonah said, "I knew that you are a gracious and compassionate God."[21] At the same time, they knew that God would not allow guilt to remain unpunished at the coming judgment. Unknown to the idol-worshiping Greeks, whose ignorance God had previously overlooked, the world was changing. God, Creator and Lord of all, was bringing history to its climax. What paradigm-changing event led to Paul's insistence on a response from his audience? (See Acts 17:30–31.)

How did the members of the Areopagus respond to Paul's good news that God had raised his appointed judge from the dead?

DID YOU KNOW?
For the Greeks, There Is No Resurrection!

Whether the members of the Areopagus were willing to admit it or not, Paul's presentation gave them much to think about. But nothing he said matched the impact of his reference to the resurrection of Jesus:

that God "has given proof of this to everyone by raising him from the dead."[22]

In fact, talking about Jesus' resurrection was the controversial subject that brought Paul to the Areopagus in the first place!

Although Greek thought was seldom monolithic, all Greek philosophy agreed that there is no resurrection of the body. The very idea offended them. The Areopagus itself was established on the certainty that resurrection does not exist. In his treatise *Eumenides*, the poet Aeschylus records Apollo's words on the legendary occasion when Athena founded the Areopagus: "But when dust has drained the blood of man, once he is slain, there is no return to life."[23]

Since the members of the Areopagus were "legends in their own minds" (as were most Hellenists), the possibility that they might be mistaken was unthinkable. The concept of one God, Creator of all, who brought about the restoration of *shalom* to the chaos of the cosmos through the death, resurrection, and ascension of his Son simply did not fit their presuppositions. In their view, if you died you stayed dead. So they refused to seriously consider Paul's claim.

3. The mention of Jesus' resurrection that puzzled the phi-
    losophers of Athens also caused chaos and conflict in
    other places it was proclaimed. Consider the following
    responses to the good news of Jesus' resurrection:
    *   The mixed response in Antioch of Pisidia (Acts 13:
        26–45, 50)

    *   When Paul addressed the Sanhedrin in Jerusalem
        (Acts 23:1–11)

    *   Paul's defense to Festus and King Agrippa
        (Acts 26:19–29)

    *   The testimony of the apostles (Acts 1:1–3, 21–22;
        2:29–41; 3:11–16; 4:1–10, 32–35; 5:29–42)

What did the fact of Jesus' resurrection reveal about who was in charge of what happened in the world, and why did many perceive it to be a dangerous idea?

4. Followers of Jesus always want the proclamation of the gospel to have a life-changing impact on people. What were the three different ways Paul's audience responded? (See Acts 17:32–34.)

Is this what you would have expected? Why or why not?

BELIEVER PROFILE
Dionysius and Damaris Believe

The power of the Holy Spirit transformed the minds and hearts of few who heard Paul's message in Athens. Just one member, Dionysius, of the hundred or so members of the Areopagus, chose to reject his Greek gods and the god of his own mind in order to follow Jesus. Yet I think that persuading just one of the intellectual elite of Athens ranks quite high on the list of miracles God's Spirit accomplished through his apostles. According to legend, Dionysius became the first bishop of Athens and was martyred by Emperor Domitian. Today he is the patron saint of Athens.

The Text also mentions a woman named Damaris who believed, which raises the question of why a woman was present during this meeting of the Areopagus. Although some philosophical schools included women, they were generally excluded from public life including the predominantly male philosophical schools. So it is likely she was one of the high-priced prostitutes known as *hetairai*, or companions, who had long-term relationships with the educated Greeks.[24] Such women provided companionship, intellectual stimulation, and sexual pleasure, and were known to frequent gatherings of the intellectual elite. If Damaris was such a companion, the miracle of her response to the gospel is as great, if not more so, than that of Dionysius.

Although there was not a strong Christian presence in Athens for hundreds of years after Paul's visit, I am inspired when I visit it today. The Parthenon still stands magnificently on the Acropolis. But below it is a major intersection of "St. Paul's Street" and "Dionysius the Areopagite Avenue"! And surrounding the ruins of the ancient agora where Paul engaged the intellectual elite are churches where people gather to celebrate the Jesus Paul proclaimed. Best of all, thousands of tourists gather at the foot of the Areopagus—Mars Hill—to read and photograph a bronze plaque embedded in the rock with Paul's address inscribed on it!

Reflection

In one sense Paul's experience in Athens was not a great success. Yes, a few believed Paul's message, but none of them are mentioned again in the Bible. There is no First and Second Athens in the Bible, nor is there evidence that Paul established a believing community there. After a few days in Athens, Paul moved on to Corinth where he had a very different experience.

So we may wonder why most of Paul's audience was not persuaded by his excellent proclamation. As I consider the mission God has given to all who follow him, I think, in part, the apparent lack of impact occurred because there wasn't a strong, living testimony of Paul's words in Athens. Remember, God calls his people to *bring* and *be* the message. Our words alone will not convince. We must illustrate our words by the lives we live. If we do not live with God as our Lord and imitate his Son Jesus in our righteousness, love, forgiveness, and compassion for the marginalized, we undermine our own testimony.

Each of us is God's Parthenon! So live big. Live public. Live with an unmistakable identity in your community that stands out like the Parthenon.

But let's do it in God's way. We don't need to shout, condemn, or criticize. We do way too much of that.

We need to speak the truth of the Text using the metaphors and experiences that people understand. We need to consider how best to communicate God's story to our own judgmental, combative, and confrontational society. We need to demonstrate the message and put God on display as we live every day and engage people who do not know God. We need to bring God's presence to those who grope for him in the dark and make him near so people can find him.

In what ways are you making God near to those who don't know him?

Which of your words and actions may be driving a wedge between God and those who don't know him?

How closely does your message match how you live every day?

What is it about the way you live that stands out for God in your world in the way the Parthenon stood out in Athens?

TURNING WEAKNESS INTO STRENGTH

When Paul proclaimed to the Areopagus the good news about the coming of God's kingdom, his ministry in Athens came to an abrupt halt. It didn't end because he had to flee for his life as he had in Antioch and Iconium (when he preached the good news that God included Gentiles in his kingdom) or Thessalonica and Berea (where the fact that crowds believed his teaching implied that Caesar wasn't king). It didn't end because the authorities thought the economic implications of the gospel threatened their security as happened in Philippi. Instead, the intellectual elite of the Roman Empire responded to Paul's masterful and rhetorically eloquent presentation of the gospel with little more than disdainful sneers or lukewarm yawns.

Although a handful of people in Athens became followers of Jesus, there are no later epistles or other indications that a community of believers was established there. Paul's intellectual understanding and brilliant, culturally aware reasoning apparently had little effect on the Athenians. So Paul left and walked toward Corinth, the next logical destination in the Greek province of Achaia. We can imagine him walking alone, seemingly discouraged, toward a city where he had no friends or resources. Perhaps, as he walked, he reflected on the response his message received in Athens and how he might share the gospel differently in Corinth.

Whatever his thoughts, Paul's approach to sharing the gospel changed dramatically when he arrived in Corinth. It seems he recognized that when God chooses human partners to participate in his great story of redemption, he often chooses the least likely candidates—the underclass, the weak, the poor, the despised, the underperformers. For example, God chose Abraham and Sarah when they were aliens wandering in a land that was not their own. He chose a nation of Hebrew slaves. He chose David, the youngest of seven brothers. He chose Mary, young and unmarried, to be the mother of Jesus. He chose a group of disciples who apparently were unqualified to follow a rabbi. As counterintuitive as God's choices may seem to us, that is how he often works. He chooses unlikely human partners, redeems them, empowers them by his Spirit, directs them by his Text, and encourages them through his community to become his witnesses and make him known to all nations.

God has always accomplished great work through his "weak" and "foolish" partners who realize how little they bring to the mission to which God has called them and depend on the mercy of his strength and provision. Somewhere between Athens and Corinth, Paul realized that his brilliant mind or powerful words could not lead people to join God's story and accept his reign in their lives. Faith rests not on human cleverness, but on God alone. As Paul stepped forward by faith in Corinth, he would learn that in human weakness God's power is revealed!

Corinth truly presented a unique challenge for Paul and the kingdom he proclaimed. This important and prosperous crossroads colony of the Roman Empire had been populated originally by freed slaves, the poor, and retired soldiers. Worship of the goddess Aphrodite brought notoriety to Corinth for its immoral lifestyle. Its reputation for affluence and immorality attracted people of every race and religious heritage and drew more unsavory characters to its streets than did other port cities. If Athens was the city where people read poetry, Corinth was the city of wild partying. If a believing community could be established in Corinth, it would be a highly visible witness of the gospel's transforming power!

Opening Thoughts (3 minutes)

The Very Words of God

I came to you in weakness with great fear and trembling. My message and my preaching were not with wise and persuasive words, but with a demonstration of the Spirit's power, so that your faith might not rest on human wisdom, but on God's power.

1 Corinthians 2:3–5

Think About It

One childhood experience seared into the memory of most kids is having to choose, or be chosen for, a team. Whether the activity was a game or a group project, two children were named as captains of opposing teams. First one, then the other, would take turns choosing the "best" of the remaining children for their team. For many kids this was a dreadful experience. One by one the strongest, fastest, smartest, or most popular kids were chosen. The last child chosen was the one no one valued or wanted on their team. Usually everyone knew who would be chosen first and who would be last.

Imagine for a moment if one team captain picked the weakest, slowest, dumbest, or most unpopular child first!

How would the rest of the group respond?

What would they think was happening?

Who might have the courage to make such a choice, and why?

Video Notes (32 minutes)

God chooses and trains his partners

Paul goes to Corinth—

In weakness, fear, and trembling

A decadent Roman colony

Erastus, exception to the rule

Paul's mission in Corinth—build a temple for God to live with his people

God provides Aquila and Priscilla

Paul goes to the Jews, then to the Gentiles

God encourages Paul

Weakness turned to strength

Our hope in weakness

Video Discussion (6 minutes)

1. Corinth was well known for its tainted social and moral reputation. However, in Paul's day it was also a strategic and prosperous city because of its identity as a Roman colony and its location between the Gulf of Corinth and the Saronic Gulf on the Aegean Sea. Discuss the types and numbers of people who either lived, traveled through, or visited Corinth for a period of time.

   • On the map, note ancient Corinth's location and the cities of Lechaion and Cenchrea where cargo from ships in the Corinthian and Saronic gulfs was unloaded and transported in carts across the isthmus and reloaded into ships on the other side. In addition to the great number of sailors and laborers needed to accomplish this task, what kind of workers would local supporting businesses employ?

   • The biannual Isthmian Games and the worship of Aphrodite (whose temples were located on the Acrocorinth as well as within the city) attracted many thousands of visitors, athletes, and pleasure seekers. What kind of impact might their experience in Corinth have when they returned home? Consider also the variety of workers needed to meet their requirements for food, shelter, and other services during their stay.

- Consider, too, that the Isthmus of Corinth provided the only land access between Athens and the mainland of Greece to the Peloponnese Peninsula of southern Greece. Corinth's location as a trading center via both land and sea brought great wealth, slaves, and goods from as far away as Egypt, Gaul, Spain, and the Middle East. As the capital of Achaia and most prosperous city in Greece, Corinth was perhaps the most important city Paul ever visited. Paul had encountered the intellectual and philosophical influencers of the Greco-Roman culture in Athens. Who were the influencers he would expect to encounter in Corinth?

2. Paul had taken the good news of Jesus to a number of cities before he headed toward Corinth. Consider the depth of knowledge, vigor, and passion with which he had approached his mission in cities such as Lystra, Pisidian Antioch, Philippi, Thessalonica, and even Athens. Then, by his own testimony, Paul left Athens and said he came to Corinth "in weakness and in fear and with much trembling" (1 Corinthians 2:3).

What had happened to the Paul who turned the world upside down in city after city, and how might his sense of inadequacy affect his ministry in a city such as Corinth?

3. In what ways does this overview of Corinth's economic, political, and social history help you to realize the challenges Paul faced in making God known there?

What would a community of Jesus followers mean to Paul as he proclaimed the gospel in that city where Satan's kingdom seemed to rule with such power?

Why would a community of faithful followers of Jesus—a temple of God—be so important to the mission of making God known in Corinth?

Small Group Bible Discovery and Discussion (15 minutes)

Paul Changes His Strategy

We might expect the religious Athenians to be more receptive to the good news of Jesus than the notoriously immoral Corinthians. That was not the case, however. Athens was the first city Paul visited in the Greek province of Achaia, and although he made a brilliant presentation of the gospel to the Areopagus, his message did not generate a strong response. He later wrote that the first community of Jesus followers established in Achaia was not in Athens but in Corinth.

We must not view Paul's ministry in Athens as a failure, however. His address to the Areopagus was superb in every way. To this day it remains an inspiring and instructive presentation of the gospel. We also know that God anointed Paul's message and a few people believed. Yet for whatever reason—the lack of response in Athens, a very different situation in Corinth, the Spirit's leading, or something else—Paul significantly changed his ministry strategy when he brought the gospel of Jesus to Corinth.

Paul no longer relied solely on his intellectual brilliance or eloquence to engage his audience. In fact, Paul states this in a letter to the believers in Corinth:

> And so it was with me, brothers and sisters. When I came to you, I did not come with eloquence or human wisdom as I proclaimed to you the testimony about God. For I resolved to know nothing while I was with you except Jesus Christ and him crucified. I came to you in weakness with great fear and trembling. My message and my preaching were not with wise and persuasive words, but with a demonstration of the Spirit's power, so that your faith might not rest on human wisdom, but on God's power.[1]

This change in perspective does not mean there is no place for brilliant, eloquent presentation of the gospel, but Paul had learned the limitations of trying to logically reason someone into the kingdom of God.

In Corinth Paul also stopped "journeying." During his first teaching tour, focused in the province of Galatia (the southwest area of modern Turkey), Paul traveled for approximately two years. He founded several churches during that time, but never stayed in any one place longer than a few weeks. He revisited the same cities at the beginning of his second tour, and then, following God's leading, moved on to the provinces of Macedonia and Achaia in Greece. In Macedonia—the cities of Philippi, Thessalonica, and Berea—and in Athens, Paul continued his established pattern of staying in a city for only a few weeks. But in Corinth, his pattern changed. Paul stayed in Corinth for about eighteen months and later spent nearly three years in Ephesus.

During Paul's extended stay in Corinth, his relationships with his "disciples" became more significant. In Lystra at the beginning of his second teaching journey, Paul had chosen Timothy as a "disciple."[2] When Paul fled Berea, Timothy stayed behind and later rejoined him in Corinth. Paul met two other "disciples" in Corinth who also played a significant role in his ministry and later ministered with him in Ephesus and Rome. Let's see how Paul's new strategy played out in Corinth.

1. From the beginning of his great redemption story, God chose human partners who were considered weak in the eyes of the world to play a key role in making him known. By his own testimony, Paul came to Corinth following that ancient pattern. Weak and inadequate for the work ahead of him, Paul had to depend on God for provision and strength to make God known in that ungodly place. How did Paul describe his weakness and need for God when he came to Corinth? (See 1 Corinthians 2:1–4.)

In what ways was Paul's view of his approach in Corinth a contrast to his experience in Athens?

2. In addition to Luke's brief account of Paul's visit to Corinth (Acts 18), Paul's extended letters to the congregation of Jesus followers he established in Corinth give us insight into his experience as God's witness there. What did Paul's weakness and inadequacy help him to realize about himself and what makes a person an effective partner in God's redemptive story? (See 1 Corinthians 4:20; 2 Corinthians 12:7–10.)

3. Paul came to Corinth in "weakness with great fear and trembling," yet showed no signs of backing away from the mission. Why? What gave him the strength to continue? As is so often the case with Paul, the Text provides helpful insight.

Paul knew the Text, and from it he not only knew his mission, but he knew that he came from a heritage of weakness that God turned to strength. It was no mystery to him that God frequently chose unlikely partners who, in and of themselves, were incapable of doing what he called them to do. Paul knew that in every seemingly impossible situation, God chose, equipped, and empowered ordinary people to do amazing things so that the world might know him. Paul must have had faith that God would turn his weakness into strength just as he had done for his Jewish ancestors.

Hebrews 11 provides a list of weak, powerless, scorned, and unlikely people whom God chose as his coworkers in redemption. The list explains the amazing things they did in serving the Lord and making him known in the world. Consider just a few examples from that "unlikely partners" list—many of their stories will be familiar to you—and discuss both what made them fearful, weak, or incapable and how God turned their weakness into strength. (You may also want to add to your list other "unlikely" partners whose weakness God turned into strength.)

Unlikely Partner(s)	References	Their Weakness Turned to Strength
Abraham, Sarah, and Isaac	Hebrews 11:8–12, 17–19; also Genesis 12; 17:1–18:15; 21:1–7; 22:1–19	
Moses and his parents	Hebrews 11:23–29; also Exodus 1:8–2:15; 3:1–15:21	
Gideon	Hebrews 11:32–34; also Judges 6–7	
David	Hebrews 11:32–34; also 1 Samuel 16–17	
Other _____		
Other _____		

FOR GREATER UNDERSTANDING
Why Corinth?

In the absence of a clear answer from Scripture, scholars have suggested many reasons as to why Paul went to Corinth following his visit to Athens. Was Corinth simply the nearest large city? Was it because Corinth had a Jewish community and synagogue? Did God's Spirit lead him there through a revelation unknown to us? We don't know. But from the perspective of Corinth being a suitable location for God's people to carry out the mission of putting God on display so that the world would come to know him, it was nearly perfect!

At Mount Sinai, God called the Hebrew people to be his partners in advancing his great plan of redemption. He gave them the mission of demonstrating his character so that all people would come to know him and experience the *shalom* of his kingdom. God's people were not only to *bring* the message of God and his kingdom but to *be* the message by demonstrating God's will and character through their words and actions in daily life. God then entrusted to his people the Promised Land, bisected by the *Via Maris*, the crossroads of the ancient world, as their platform for making him known.

At times God's people were faithful to the mission. At other times they fell short. But God's plan of redemption continued to move forward with the coming of Jesus. By his atoning death and resurrection, Jesus made possible for all people a restored relationship with God our Creator. By his every word and action, Jesus embodied the mission perfectly, putting God on display and demonstrating his true character and love for all people. Before his ascension to heaven, Jesus entrusted the same mission—the mission God gave to Israel at Mount Sinai—to his followers. As a follower of Jesus, Paul went out into the world—first to the Jews, then to the Gentiles—bringing the good news that Jesus had come and offering hope by displaying what life looks like when God reigns.

Although we can't state specifically why Paul went to Corinth, several unique characteristics made it a strategic location for carrying out his mission:

- Corinth was a crossroads city! Just as people from all over the world traveled through the Promised Land, people traveled through Corinth. It was on the major east-west sea route linking Rome with eastern parts of the Roman Empire. It was also on the main north-south land route connecting the Peloponnese Peninsula to mainland Greece. If people in Corinth believed and lived in a way that demonstrated what God is like, the gospel message would spread throughout the Roman Empire.[3]

- A large Jewish community lived in Corinth. Paul consistently began his teaching in the local synagogue where Jews and God-fearing Gentiles who knew and accepted the Text would readily understand his message. Although Jewish communities at times opposed Paul's message that Jesus was Messiah, Savior, and Lord, they had influence in the Roman Empire. If they believed Paul's interpretation of the Text, their witness in word and example would impact the local community and beyond.

- Paul's visit to Corinth coincided with the biannual Isthmian Games. This event, held in honor of the god Poseidon, was nearly as important as the Olympic Games. It drew thousands of athletes and visitors to Corinth, providing significant opportunities to spread the gospel message to the far reaches of the Roman Empire. The games also created a demand for temporary shelter—a good business opportunity for tentmakers such as Paul and his friends and co-laborers, Aquila and Priscilla.

- Immorality associated with idol worship was so common in the Roman Empire that it often wasn't even thought of as being "immoral." The immorality of Corinth, however, acquired worldwide notoriety. The display of excessive wealth, drunkenness, and indulgence in every kind of human pleasure-seeking made Corinth a cesspool of human vice. Could any place in the Roman Empire be less promising for the gospel message to take root? But what if that community truly became living proof of God's kingdom? Imagine the countercultural statement a community that lived by moral restraint, sexual purity, sobriety, and compassion for others would make in Corinth!

4. Intellectual arguments and logical reasoning can be important tools for making God known. But an examination of the Text shows that is not the way God instructed Israel to carry out the mission of bringing lost nations into his kingdom. Rather, God called his people to be living witnesses, a kingdom of priests whose lives portrayed by their words and actions who he was, what he had done, and what his *shalom* looks like in practice. The everyday lives of God's people, not the logic of their words, were to be the living proof that their testimony was true!

In Athens there apparently was no community of God's people to be the living proof of Paul's words, no living example in words and action of what redemption and *shalom* looked like that people who did not know God could observe. That would change in Corinth! But how do God's people know what it looks like to be living proof of God's kingdom on earth? Let's consider what the Text says:

a. How did God describe the role he wanted Israel, as his chosen people, to play in the world, and how similar is it to the instructions Jesus gave to his followers? (See Exodus 19:1–6; 1 Peter 2:9–12.)

b. How do God's people not only make God known but also increase his reputation in the world? (See 1 Chronicles 16:8; Matthew 6:9–10.)

DID YOU KNOW?
To "Hallow" God's Name

In ancient times, names were more than just what a person was called. Names described a person's reputation and character. To "hallow" God's name meant to add honor and glory to his character and reputation by the things you said and did. It is the opposite of "profane," which means to diminish the reputation of one's name or to empty it of honor and significance. To "hallow" God's name (*kiddush ha shem* in Hebrew) is really the positive expression of the command "you shall not take my name in vain" (*hillul ha shem*).

    c.   A witness is someone who declares what he or she has seen or experienced. What do God's people need to know or experience in order to be his witnesses? (See Isaiah 43:10–13; Acts 10:36–42.)

    d.   What does God want his people to be in the world, and what happens when they are? (See Isaiah 42:6–7; Matthew 5:14–16.)

    e.   When people who do not know God interact with God's people, what should they experience? (See Exodus 25:8; Acts 2:1–4; 1 Corinthians 3:16.)

Faith Lesson (3 minutes)

In God's hands, human weaknesses accomplish his purposes beautifully! God is glorified and his people learn that they can depend on him. When we fall flat on our faces, when we experience epic failures, we are forced to realize that we can't be successful in our own strength. We are forced to lean into God's strength. And when God accomplishes the "impossible," it is evident that he—and no other person or power—deserves the credit.

God consistently uses the weakness of his partners in redemption to demonstrate his strength and bring glory to his name. The greatest example of God's strength in human weakness is Jesus himself. Throughout his life on earth, Jesus accepted the limitations of human life and his dependence on the Father. He experienced hunger, pain, sorrow, weariness, hardship, misunderstanding, and rejection. In his ultimate display of "weakness," Jesus was nailed to a cross. As his life slipped away, not even his Father in heaven would help him.

Yet that was the moment of victory, the moment "God chose the weak things of the world to shame the strong."[4] Because of Jesus' death and resurrection, God's glory exploded, unloosing the chokehold the Evil One held on God's creation! This paradigm-changing event beckons all of creation to lift up praise, glory, and honor to God and God alone. And it happened because Jesus, who "was crucified in weakness . . . lives by God's power!"[5]

1. When Paul went to Corinth in weakness, fear, and trembling, whatever would be accomplished for God's kingdom would be to God's honor because it could not happen any other way. We may have good intentions to show God's power and bring him glory, but we often attempt to do it in our own strength. We turn down opportunities to do God's work because we "aren't gifted that way." Perhaps we need to seriously consider whose glory we want to make known. How willing, for example, are we to be

humbled—to face such an impossible task that we are
overwhelmed by our weakness and fear—so that God's
power will be made perfect through us and bring glory,
honor, and praise to his name?

2. Only when we recognize our weakness and inability to
    accomplish what God has called us to do and be will his
    strength empower us. As long as we think we are able to
    act on God's behalf, we are not open to being used by
    him. It is easy to say we want to trust in God's strength,
    but it is quite difficult to do it. Yet we must put ourselves
    in God's hands every day. As a Jewish friend of mine
    often says, "Plan to do at least one thing every day you
    cannot do without God's help." Are you willing to take
    that step? What one thing will you do today that you can
    accomplish only by God's strength and power?

Closing (1 minute)

Read 2 Corinthians 12:9–10 aloud together: "But he said to me,
'My grace is sufficient for you, for my power is made perfect in
weakness.' Therefore I will boast all the more gladly about my
weaknesses, so that Christ's power may rest on me. That is why,
for Christ's sake, I delight in weaknesses, in insults, in hardships,
in persecutions, in difficulties. For when I am weak, then I am
strong."

Then pray, praising God that he is the all-loving, faithful, almighty God who through the death and resurrection of Jesus has paid the ultimate sacrifice in order to offer forgiveness and restoration to all of his lost children. Thank him for restoring you to his family, his *beth ab*, and inviting you to be his partner in redeeming those who do not yet know him. Ask him for a humble, committed, trusting heart that is not afraid to be weak or inadequate for the task ahead. Pray for a heart that pursues the mission for the honor and glory of God.

Memorize

> *But he said to me, "My grace is sufficient for you, for my power is made perfect in weakness." Therefore I will boast all the more gladly about my weaknesses, so that Christ's power may rest on me. That is why, for Christ's sake, I delight in weaknesses, in insults, in hardships, in persecutions, in difficulties. For when I am weak, then I am strong.*

2 Corinthians 12:9–10

Making God Known in a Broken World

In-Depth Personal Study Sessions

Study 1 | Paul Was Weak, But God Had a Plan

The Very Words of God

> *After this, Paul left Athens and went to Corinth. There he met a Jew named Aquila, a native of Pontus, who had recently come from Italy with his wife Priscilla, because Claudius had ordered all Jews to leave Rome. Paul went to see them, and because he was a tentmaker as they were, he stayed and worked with them.*
>
> Acts 18:1–3

Bible Discovery

Paul Was Not Alone

In early 51 AD, when Paul walked alone up Lechaion Street into Corinth, he stepped into the boomtown of the Roman Empire. Corinth was a major center for commerce and trade, and had one of the largest slave markets in the Roman world. It was also the object of continued development and building by the Roman emperors—Julius Caesar, Tiberius, Claudius, and others—who provided significant funding for an imperial temple, theater, aqueduct, and other civic, commercial, and religious structures in order to showcase Roman culture in Corinth.

In addition to its busy and powerful economic and political environment, thousands of people from every province of the empire streamed into Corinth seeking the pleasures of the good life. The city was awash in wealth and every known human vice. The professor I studied with in Greece described it as "one enormous tavern and brothel."

For Paul, feeling weak and inadequate after his difficult and disappointing experience in Athens, the challenges of sharing the gospel message in Corinth must have been intimidating. Nevertheless, he continued to move forward with the mission to which God had called him. Soon he would discover that he was not as alone and inadequate as he feared. Yes, he was weak in his own strength, but God had been working in Corinth ahead of him! God had already put into place everything Paul needed to make God's message known and to be a living example of what life looks like when God reigns.

1. Paul may have walked into Corinth thinking he was the only follower of Jesus in that city of many thousands of people. Who in that mass of humanity did Paul encounter shortly after his arrival, and what do you think that meant to him? (See Acts 18:1–3.)

    In what ways did that relationship strengthen Paul in terms of his:
    • Ministry of making the good news of Jesus known?

    • Having a place to live?

    • Finding work to provide for his material needs?

- Desire to establish a kingdom of priests whose everyday lives would display God's character for the world to see?

PROFILE OF PAUL'S PARTNERS IN MINISTRY
Aquila and Priscilla

Shortly after Paul arrived in Corinth, he met a couple of tentmakers, a husband and wife named Aquila and Priscilla. They apparently were successful enough to have their own shop with living quarters above, as was typical of many shops in Corinth. What is most intriguing about them is how they came to be in Corinth when Paul arrived.

Aquila was a Jew from Pontus, a city near the Black Sea in what today is Turkey. His name is actually Roman and means "eagle," which he possibly

THIS RECONSTRUCTED, VAULTED SHOP WAS TYPICAL OF THE TWO-STORY SHOPS THAT LINED THE PERIMETER OF CORINTH'S AGORA. BUSINESS GENERALLY WAS CONDUCTED ON THE GROUND LEVEL, AND THE FAMILY LIVED ON THE UPPER LEVEL.

acquired through military service or as a former slave. Priscilla, a Gentile, may have been a family member or a manumitted slave of a well-known patrician family in Rome.

The couple had lived in Rome and likely came to Corinth shortly before Paul did as a result of the 48 AD riots in Rome that may have been caused by disagreement in the Jewish community over a certain "Chrestus." Apparently the issue was whether Jesus was the Christ, the promised Messiah. In response, Emperor Claudius expelled the Jews from Rome[6] for disturbing the peace.[7]

When they were expelled from Rome, the Jewish community obviously suffered economically, politically, and physically. Yet this event turned out to be an amazing example of God's provision for Paul and preparation for the arrival of the gospel message in Corinth. Of all the places Aquila and Priscilla could have gone, they chose Corinth. Of all the people in Corinth Paul could have met, he met husband and wife tentmakers who were deeply committed to Jesus.[8]

What an encouragement Aquila and Priscilla must have been to Paul after the meager response he received in Athens! In Paul's weakness, with no friends, no money, no job, and no place to gather with those who wanted to hear his message, God's strength was at work. By God's gracious provision, Paul found an established couple who were ready to give him a place to work and live and—more important—share their common bond as committed, faithful followers of Jesus. They were willing to be faithful participants in God's redemption story and became Paul's coworkers who supported his ministry for the rest of his life.

2. Aquila and Priscilla's appearance in Paul's life is nothing short of amazing. Their ability to provide a place for Paul to live and work as well as their companionship in faith and vocation no doubt was encouraging to Paul. Who could have imagined that in Corinth Paul would find the couple who would become the most prominent couple in the development of the early church? Consider what

the Bible tells us about how God provided support and encouragement for Paul and the early church through Paul's ongoing relationship with Aquila and Priscilla.

a. As it turned out, Paul spent significant time with Priscilla and Aquila in Corinth. What happened when Paul left Corinth to go to Ephesus? (See Acts 18:18–19.)

b. What important role(s) did Aquila and Priscilla have in the community of Jesus followers in Ephesus? (See Acts 18:24–26; 1 Corinthians 16:19.)

c. How highly did Paul value Aquila and Priscilla both personally and for their contribution to the growth of the early Christian church? (See Romans 16:3–5.)

3. Paul came to Corinth alone, intending to proclaim the gospel "not [by] eloquence or human wisdom," as he had in Athens, but with a firm resolution to "know nothing . . . except Jesus Christ and him crucified."[9] Paul did not end up working alone in Corinth. God provided several followers of Jesus, united in the same mission to advance God's kingdom.

a. God provided Paul's coworkers, Priscilla and Aquila, who played an important role as "shepherds" of house churches in three of the most significant centers of the Jesus movement outside Israel—Corinth first, then Ephesus, and later Rome. In Corinth, what was Paul able to do to accomplish his mission after he met them? (See Acts 18:3–4.)

b. Who else did God provide for companionship and support while Paul was in Corinth, and what did they enable Paul to do? (See Acts 18:5.)

How important was their support to Paul's understanding of what God wanted him to accomplish in Corinth? (See 1 Corinthians 2:1–5.)

PROFILE OF PAUL'S PARTNERS IN MINISTRY
Timothy and Silas

Certainly Paul's acquaintance with Aquila and Priscilla encouraged him greatly. Through their presence and resources God provided a job and place for Paul to stay as well as a setting for sharing the good news and a place for the fledgling church to meet. God's strength was at work in Paul's weakness, providing far beyond what he could have asked or imagined. Then more good news arrived: Timothy and Silas showed up!

When Paul first began his teaching journeys, he does not appear to have had any disciples, which is unusual. A rabbi typically selected disciples to follow him and learn from him—not just by hearing what the rabbi taught but by imitating the rabbi's every action. During Paul's second teaching journey he visited Lystra, where he had taught two years earlier, and chose Timothy to be his disciple.[10]

The son of a Gentile father and a Jewish mother, Timothy was an unlikely disciple. He was a *mamzer*, the child of a forbidden marriage. As such, he was uncircumcised and remained an outsider to the Jewish community. However, Timothy spent many years with Paul and became one of his most trusted friends and coworkers. In his letter to the Philippians, Paul honored Timothy by explaining "that Timothy has proved himself, because as a son with his father he has served with me in the work of the gospel."[11]

Paul and Timothy had labored together in Philippi, Thessalonica, and Berea. When Paul had to leave Berea due to opposition, Timothy stayed behind to continue the mission. After Timothy rejoined Paul in Corinth, they taught together for nearly two years. Then Timothy joined Paul in Ephesus where they worked together for an additional three years. For much of the time Paul was imprisoned in Rome, Timothy attended to his needs, and when Paul realized his time to live was short he asked Timothy to join him during his final days in prison.

Although we know less about Silas than we do Timothy, he played an important role in Paul's ministry too. The church elders in Jerusalem selected Silas to join Paul on his second teaching journey because he "said much to encourage and strengthen the believers."[12] What a wonderful reputation to have! His sudden appearance in Corinth when Paul was feeling weak, fearful, and inadequate is a striking example of God being strong in our weakness.

Silas was with Paul from the beginning of his second teaching journey. He was imprisoned with Paul in Philippi and continued with him to Thessalonica and Berea, where he remained when Paul went to Athens. After Silas and Timothy rejoined Paul in Corinth, the three of them preached the good news of Jesus the Messiah. Silas is not mentioned in Luke's account of Paul's life after Paul moved on to Ephesus, so he likely remained in Corinth.

At a time when Paul was struggling to continue on with the mission of making God known to the Gentile world, God answered his weakness. In Timothy and Silas, God brought exactly the people Paul needed to assist him. The encouragement of their partnership in ministry turned Paul's weakness into strength.

4. God's provision for Paul in Corinth was amazing. It began when Paul met Aquila and Priscilla, the tentmakers and disciples of Jesus, and was further strengthened when Silas and Timothy rejoined him. But God's provision for Paul got even better.

a. Paul had taught in Thessalonica for only a brief time before conflict with the kingdom of this world erupted in a riot that forced him to flee in the middle of the night. What good news did Timothy and Silas bring about how God had anointed Paul's efforts to make Jesus known in that pro-Roman city that tolerated no king other than Caesar? (See 1 Thessalonians 1:4–9; 3:6–8.)

b. Timothy and Silas also brought a gift from the believers in Philippi. In what ways did this gift not only
encourage Paul but help to advance God's kingdom
as well? (See Acts 18:5; 2 Corinthians 11:9; Philippians
4:14–16.)

Reflection

Paul's ministry in Corinth provides a powerful lesson of encouragement. He came in weakness to what appeared to be the
least likely place to make God known. With nothing of himself
to offer, he made himself available to God's strength. And God
responded in ways that were far beyond what Paul could ask or
imagine. Through the power of God's strength at work in him,
Paul became strong, and God's kingdom came to Corinth as it
does in heaven!

Paul experienced what God promises to everyone who believes
and joins God's great redemption story. The question we have to
answer is, will we join the story and live it every day?

Will we recognize the mission God has given to us and,
despite our weaknesses and inadequacy, step forward to do
what God has called us to do and live as his kingdom of
priests in a broken world? How deep is your commitment to
do this?

Are we willing to admit our weaknesses and failures in being examples of what life looks like when God reigns? What are your areas of weakness, fear, and inadequacy in relationship to displaying who God is in your family, your community, your vocation, your recreational activities, your politics, your causes, and every other area of life?

Will we trust God to provide whatever we need as his partners in the great redemption story?

What do you need to trust God to provide for you, as his partner in your weakness today?

What is your commitment to continue to move forward, pursuing the mission and trusting that Paul's triumphant declaration in Ephesians 3:20–21 will be yours as well?

Study 2 | Paul Makes Jesus Known in Corinth

The Very Words of God

> *One night the Lord spoke to Paul in a vision: "Do not be afraid; keep on speaking, do not be silent. For I am with you, and no one is going to attack and harm you, because I have many people in this city." So Paul stayed in Corinth for a year and a half, teaching them the word of God.*

Acts 18:9–11

Bible Discovery

Paul Goes First to the Jews

Of all the cities in the Roman Empire, Corinth was as spiritually broken as any. The chaos of the kingdom of this world ruled in drunkenness, sexual immorality, greed, material consumption, and most every other human indulgence. Yet even there Paul found a thriving Jewish congregation where he could begin telling others about God's plan of redemption made possible through the shed blood of Jesus, the promised Messiah.

The Jewish congregation in Corinth, the community of God's people who already were committed to the mission of making God known to the nations, surely encouraged Paul. They already believed that the Text was God's inspired revelation. They already knew how the Text described the Messiah's coming, and they eagerly anticipated it. That motivated community of people who knew the Scriptures was the ideal starting point to begin sharing the good news that Jesus, Messiah, had come.

Paul came to Corinth in weakness, committed to nothing more than sharing the message of Jesus. And that was all he needed. God had provided a way for Paul to work at his trade with Aquila and Priscilla—a couple who followed Jesus as he did! God had prepared a synagogue where Paul could worship and reason with the Jewish community on the Sabbath. Let's see how God's power continued to make Paul strong when he began sharing the message of Jesus.

1. In the cities he visited, Paul went to the Jewish synagogue
    to present the gospel message before he presented it any-
    where else. What eagerly awaited hope did Paul share with
    every Jewish community, and why was that hope important
    to God's plan of redemption? (See Acts 13:32–39; 26:6–8.)

The synagogue community in Corinth included Jews and
non-Jews—called God-fearers or God-fearing Gentiles,
who had renounced their pagan faith and believed in
and worshiped the God of the Hebrew Bible. Why did
Paul "reason" with the synagogue community about Jesus
being the Messiah before he took the gospel message to
others? (See Acts 26:22–23; Romans 1:16; 3:1–2.)

Since Mount Sinai, where God called the Hebrews to be
partners in his great redemption story, God has intended for
his people to live as his kingdom of priests who represent
his presence and display his character to the world. He has
wanted the community of his people to make him known
by the way they live and interact with others so that people
who don't know God will be drawn to him and want to join
his kingdom. How important would an established community of Jesus followers be in making God and his plan of
redemption known to the Gentiles of Corinth?

A CARVED MARBLE ARCH SEGMENT DECORATED WITH MENORAHS, PALM BRANCHES, AND CITRONS PROVIDES PHYSICAL EVIDENCE OF A JEWISH CONGREGATION IN CORINTH. ARCHAEOLOGISTS HAVE ALSO FOUND A STONE LINTEL WITH A HEBREW INSCRIPTION "SYNAGOGUE OF THE HEBREWS." ALTHOUGH BOTH OF THESE PIECES DATE AFTER THE TIME OF PAUL, THEY CONFIRM THE PRESENCE OF A JEWISH COMMUNITY IN THAT PAGAN CITY.

2. Sabbath worship in the synagogue community, which the Jews called "prayer," typically involved listening to the reading and explanation of the Scriptures, recitation and singing of psalms, and saying the *shema* and the prayers for the day. Following worship, teachers from the community or visiting teachers were invited to lead a discussion on the Torah. Paul typically participated in such discussions.

Luke often used the Greek word *dielexato* (translated as "reason with" in English) to describe Paul's interaction or discussion with Jews and God-fearing Gentiles in the synagogue. *Dielexato* does not mean to "preach" or "proclaim." Rather, it describes the rabbinic practice of dialogue with an audience in which the speaker presents his point of view and supports it by interpretations of various Hebrew Texts. In this format, the teacher would discuss and debate a number of Scripture passages that supported the point he desired to make. The teacher's synagogue audience, in turn, was well-versed in the Text and could evaluate the legitimacy of the teacher's message. We know that Paul was a brilliant scholar of the Text, so we would expect him to make a convincing case for his interpretations.

a. What was Paul's number one message to the Jewish community? (See Acts 18:4–5.)

b. How did Paul go about convincing the Jewish community of the truth of his message? (See 1 Corinthians 2:1–5.)

On what did Paul want them to base their faith? On whose power and strength did Paul realize the outcome of his message rested?

c. What impact did Paul's "reasoning" in the synagogue have on some who heard him? (See Acts 18:7–8.)

DID YOU KNOW?
Paul "Reasoned" in the Synagogue

We know Paul came to Corinth with the good news of Jesus and that his message to the synagogue community focused on Jesus being the Messiah.[13] He apparently communicated this message to his audience of Jews and God-fearing Gentiles through the familiar rabbinic method of "reasoning" or dialoging about his chosen subject using the authority and insight of the Hebrew Scriptures. Unfortunately, most followers of Jesus today have no idea what the Bible means when it says Paul "reasoned" in the synagogue. So consider the following options.

Paul may have "reasoned" through his point that Jesus is the Messiah by inserting the name of Jesus into passages of the Text that refer to the Messiah. The Western text[14] of Acts 18:4 reflects this practice, adding a phrase to Luke's account: "he [Paul] reasoned in the synagogue '*inserting the name of the Lord Jesus as the Scriptures were read.*'" This clarifying practice was well known in the Jewish community. For example, the reading of the Hebrew Text was sometimes accompanied by an Aramaic version called the *Targum.* In the *Targum*, the word "Messiah" was inserted into the text of Messianic passages. Isaiah 11:1, which reads, "A shoot will come up from the stump of Jesse," might read in the *Targum*, "The *Messiah* will come from the stump of Jesse."

It is likely that the Western text tradition accurately describes how Paul was "reasoning." He may have inserted the name "Jesus" into passages that referred to the Messiah, thereby showing that Jesus was what the passage described and, therefore, was the Messiah. We can almost hear him reading from Isaiah 7:14, "the virgin will conceive and give birth to a son," then repeating the line: "the virgin will conceive and give birth to Jesus."[15] Whatever method he used, God's power was at work in Paul's weakness and many people, including the head of the synagogue,[16] became followers of Jesus.

3. Of course, the work of making God known and the
   expansion of God's kingdom in this world does not go
   unopposed. After Silas and Timothy arrived in Corinth,
   "Paul devoted himself exclusively to preaching, testifying
   to the Jews that Jesus was the Messiah." As Paul intensi-
   fied his efforts, what also occurred? (See Acts 18:5–6.)

Luke does not explain why some Jews opposed Paul's
message, but since Paul was "reasoning" with them from
the Scriptures about Jesus, it is likely opposition came
from those who did not accept his interpretation of
the Text. However, Luke uses the word *blasphemeo* to
describe how their opposition "became abusive." *Blasphemeo* implies a personal attack or insult. How did Paul
then respond to the Jews who abusively opposed him?
(See Acts 18:6.)

What was the nature of the opposition that previously
took place in the Jewish community of Antioch of Pisidia
and led Paul to respond in a similar way? (See Acts 13:44–
51.)

Always a student of the Text, Paul's response to Jewish opposition is an allusion to the Lord's warning to Ezekiel regarding each person's accountability to either proclaim or respond appropriately to what God says. What are the responsibilities of a person who has a message from the Lord to share, and what are the responsibilities of the one who hears the message? (See Ezekiel 3:16–19; 33:4.)

DID YOU KNOW?
Paul "Shook Out His Clothes"

The Jewish gesture of shaking out one's clothes or shaking the dust off one's feet appears to have originated with Nehemiah when he called God's people to recommit to faithfulness in their walk with God.[17] When Jesus sent out his disciples, he commanded them to use this symbolic gesture if a Jewish town refused to accept their message.[18] Generally, people understood the gesture to be a testimony against those who heard, but refused to accept, the Word of God.

Paul's additional statement to the Jews in Corinth who opposed him, "Your blood be on your own heads! I am innocent of it,"[19] was another symbolic way to indicate he had fulfilled his responsibility to share God's Word with them. Paul, therefore, would be innocent of their blood if they rejected God's message. Because of their stubbornness to believe the Hebrew Scriptures, Paul would have nothing more to do with them and was free to focus his attention on making the good news of Jesus known to the Gentiles. So Paul continued his teaching next door to the synagogue, in the home of Titius Justus, a Gentile God-fearer who accepted Paul's teaching.

4. Those who opposed Paul in the synagogue of Corinth did not give up the fight easily. Not satisfied for Paul simply to leave the synagogue and focus his teaching on the Gentiles, what serious charge did they bring against him in the Roman court? (See Acts 18:12–13.)

Previously, in Philippi, Paul had faced the Roman place of judgment, the *bema* in the marketplace (*agora* in Greek, *forum* in Latin). As the official location of the city's political administration, whatever was pronounced from the *bema* was indisputable as the official application of Roman law. What does Paul's experience before the officials at the *bema*, or judgment seat, in the marketplace of Philippi reveal about what could have awaited Paul in Corinth? (See Acts 16:19–24.)

THE BEMA IN THE AGORA OF CORINTH, WHERE GALLIO, PROCONSUL OF ACHAIA, REFUSED TO PASS JUDGMENT ON THE COMPLAINT BROUGHT BY THE JEWS WHO OPPOSED PAUL

As it turned out, Gallio, who served as Roman proconsul of Achaia from 51–52 AD, heard the complaint about Paul. Gallio was the older brother of Seneca, the philosopher who at the time was the tutor and close associate of Nero, who became the Roman Emperor in 54 AD. So Gallio was a powerful person in the Roman Empire. How did Paul defend himself against the charges, and what was Gallio's unexpected response? (See Acts 18:14–16.)

Although Gallio's response was good news for Paul and the growing community of Jesus followers in Corinth (and beyond), what impact did it have on the local synagogue community? (See Acts 18:17.)

THINK ABOUT IT
God's Protection from an Unexpected Source
Since the time of Julius Caesar, Judaism had been a legal religion in the Roman Empire. Anti-Semitism was not uncommon, but Rome acknowledged the right to practice the Jewish faith and generally protected Jews from persecution. An edict of Emperor Claudius affirmed these rights while Paul was in Corinth: "It is proper that the Jews through[out] the world under Roman rule should keep their native customs without hindrance."[20] The charges brought against Paul in Corinth appear to accuse him of violating Roman law by introducing ideas that violated Jewish law and, therefore, were ideas of a different, illegal, and unprotected cult (the followers of Jesus).

God's protection of Paul when he faced these threatening charges is nothing short of amazing. Gallio's refusal to pass judgment on the charges against Paul was more than a gift of protection for him. The ruling made Christianity a protected religion under the umbrella of lawful Jewish practice. If Gallio had ruled that Paul was violating Roman law, it would have created significant problems for Paul and for Jesus followers throughout the Roman Empire. His ruling that Paul was not in violation of the law allowed followers of Jesus to practice their faith freely for some time to come.

5. In all that happened to Paul, God faithfully provided his strength and power to meet Paul's weakness and inadequacy as a witness for Jesus in Corinth. Even so, the opposition Paul faced remained difficult. It seems that Paul may have struggled to know how—or perhaps if—he should continue his mission. Was his life in danger? Should he continue speaking? Was it time to flee? What did God do to make the path ahead clear for Paul? (See Acts 18:9–11.)

In Luke's accounts, "Lord" refers to Jesus himself. How important would it have been for Paul to receive the promise that Jesus—his Redeemer and Lord who had met him on the road to Damascus and given him the very mission he was pursuing—was with him and would protect him?

Paul knew the Hebrew Text. When he heard the "I am with you" promise, he likely remembered the stories of God's faithful servants in the past who received the same promise when they felt weak, fearful, or inadequate for the task God had given to them. What encouragement do you think Paul would have received from their stories? (See Genesis 26:1–6; 31:1–3; Exodus 3:10–12; Joshua 1:1–5, 9; Isaiah 41:10; 43:1–5; Jeremiah 1:6–8.)

THINK ABOUT IT
When Our Own Strength Fails, God Is Enough

Elijah, like Paul, was a powerhouse of faithful, against-all-odds pursuit of God's calling on his life. As Paul encountered great challenges when he faced the kings and kingdoms of this world that lived by the values of the Evil One, God's prophet Elijah encountered great challenges—inspired by the same enemy of God—when he opposed King Ahab and Queen Jezebel and the idolatry they encouraged in Israel. Both men experienced remarkable "victories" in their pursuit of God's mission, and they faced moments of overwhelming discouragement and fear.

After Elijah called on God to stop the rain in Israel, it did not rain for three and a half years. Still, Israel persisted in idolatry. Elijah arranged a confrontation with the pagan Ba'al cult to show which deity could send fire to consume an offering. Israel watched as the priests of Ba'al could do nothing to inspire their god to act. Then Elijah prayed to God. Lightning fell, consumed the offering, the altar, and the water that had been poured over it, and the people were moved to declare that the Lord is God! They then slaughtered the 850 prophets of Ba'al and Asherah, and God sent rain to their land.

The result of this great victory for Elijah? Queen Jezebel promised to kill him. Elijah fled into the wilderness and told God, "I have had enough,"[21] and fell asleep. God sent an angel to provide food and drink for his weary servant. Once strengthened, Elijah walked for forty days to Horeb, the mountain of God, to talk.

God responded to Elijah's fear by assuring him he was not the only person left in Israel who was faithful to God. In fact, there were 7,000 faithful people in Israel! Encouraged, Elijah returned to his role as God's prophet in Israel. In a strikingly similar way, God came to Paul in a vision. He told Paul not to be afraid for he was not alone. There were many more of God's people in Corinth. Encouraged that God was with him, Paul continued his work of bringing the message of God's kingdom to the people of the city. I am sure it is possible that Paul who, like Elijah, had gone to the desert of Sinai, recognized the similarity of God's reassurance to him to God's reassurance of Elijah.

6. When we, as followers of Jesus, receive God's strength and see his power anoint our efforts to advance his kingdom with significant results, we tend to take credit for what God has done through us. It is easy to begin thinking that we are strong and able. What caution and testimony did Paul offer to his fellow believers that shows he remained dependent on God's strength, not his own? (See Romans 12:3; 2 Corinthians 12:9–10.)

Reflection

Jesus, the anointed King of God's kingdom, invites everyone to accept his reign so that his will is done and his kingdom comes on earth as it is in heaven. When Jesus died on the cross and rose from the dead, he defeated the Evil One, the lord of the kingdom of this world, but Satan has not given up. He continues to entice and seduce all of humanity to accept his reign and do his will, resulting in chaos that destroys the perfection and harmony of God's creation.

So it was important for Paul, as it is for followers of Jesus today, to realize that God's provision and constant presence with his people does not end the conflict. In spite of all the ways God's strength became Paul's strength and God's power convinced pagan hearts to turn to Jesus and accept his reign, Paul still faced opposition. On his own he was still too weak and inadequate to handle the task God had called him to do.

In response to Paul's need, God did not remind Paul of his training or accomplishments. He did not remind Paul of his natural gifts or learned skills. None of those would equip Paul to handle the situation. Instead, God promised, "I will be with you," and demonstrated his power by protecting Paul and working through his weakness to provide strength and success during the time Paul was in Corinth.

We live in a self-serving, pleasure-seeking culture not unlike that of Corinth. Those of us who by faith have joined God's great redemption story are his partners, chosen to demonstrate by our lives the reality of his kingdom. We can learn much from Paul's experience in Corinth. At times, fulfilling our mission in our lost culture will seem impossible, and we will feel weak, inadequate, and fearful. The most important question during those times is, "Where will we seek our strength?"

> Where do you find strength for the mission God has called you to pursue?

> In what ways do you depend on any of the following: your abilities? your economic resources? your political connections? your experience? your "good" character?

To what extent does your strength and hope rest solely on God's promise, "I will be with you"?

Study 3 | An Unlikely Community

The Very Words of God

> *Brothers and sisters, think of what you were when you were called. Not many of you were wise by human standards; not many were influential; not many were of noble birth. But God chose the foolish things of the world to shame the wise; God chose the weak things of the world to shame the strong. God chose the lowly things of this world and the despised things—and the things that are not—to nullify the things that are, so that no one may boast before him. It is because of him that you are in Christ Jesus, who has become for us wisdom from God—that is, our righteousness, holiness and redemption.*
>
> *1 Corinthians 1:26–30*

Bible Discovery

The House Church of Corinth Grows

It is hard to imagine any less promising place in Paul's world for a small community of believers to grow, mature, and make an impact than in Corinth. Given the past lifestyle and experiences of many of its members, it is nothing short of God's miracle that a house church formed, much less thrived. Paul came into the decadent city of Corinth where every pagan religion, every philosophy, every vice, and every immoral pursuit was known and practiced. He came alone, feeling weak and inadequate, knowing the fierce opposition his message had aroused in Macedonia, but not yet knowing how God had blessed his witness there.

But Corinth was ready to receive Paul's message because God had been at work. Just as God chose Hebrew slaves who had no land or country and raised them up to be his people, he chose the unlikely people of Corinth to become partners in his redemption story. In his final address to the Israelites, Moses bluntly reminded them that God did not choose them because of their importance but because he loved them and had a mission for them if they would join his story.[22] In a similar way, Paul reminded the Corinthian believers exactly who they were:[23]

> Brothers and sisters, think of what you were when you were called. Not many of you were wise by human standards, not many were influential; not many were of noble birth. But God chose the foolish things of the world to shame the wise; God chose the weak things of the world to shame the strong. God chose the lowly things of this world and the despised things—and the things that are not—to nullify the things that are, so that no one may boast before him.

That's not the kind of lineup one would want to start a business, an organization, or a team—and certainly not a church! But God often chooses unlikely partners. He is an expert at turning human weakness into strength. By the power of his Spirit, a community of Jesus followers was born and thrived in Corinth. That community stood out like a city on a hill, a light to the world that put God on display so that people would come to know him and join his redemption story too.

1. Paul was acutely aware of his weakness and inadequacy when he walked into Corinth to share the good news of Jesus in that "impossibly" difficult city. Yet God had prepared the way for Paul. Through Paul's faithful commitment to the mission and dependence on God's strength, God orchestrated an amazing demonstration of his power. During Paul's eighteen months in Corinth—by far the longest stay of his ministry to that point—his work prospered as never before. The people of Corinth heard the message and saw the kingdom of God lived out by the community of Jesus followers. How did Paul's venture in

Corinth begin, and what essentials of life and ministry had God provided for him? (See Acts 18:1–4.)

PROFILE OF A LIVING WITNESS
Tentmaking and Paul's Mission

Paul's view of life and ministry was quite different from our typical understanding. In keeping with the rabbinic tradition of his time, Paul chose to practice a trade to support himself rather than teach the Torah for financial gain. At the same time, the manner in which he conducted himself in his occupation was essential to his ministry because everything he did was to reflect God's character and demonstrate what life looked like when God was in charge. At risk of oversimplification, a Jewish teacher once described the difference in viewpoints this way: "For a Jew, God's story is a way to live. The Greeks turned it into a philosophy, the Romans into an organization, the Europeans into a culture, and the Americans into a business!" It is helpful to understand some of the ways Paul's occupation allowed him to be a living witness for God in Corinth.

- Paul's trade was that of a tentmaker, *skenopoios* in Greek, which literally means "leather worker."[24] At the time, leather was used for tents and awnings, sails for ships, harnesses, and clothing. Paul likely made and repaired all of these items and may have worked with wool and linen as well. His tools were simple and portable: knives, needles, awls, a sharpening stone, and oil for treating leather, so Paul could take the tools of his trade wherever he traveled.

- At the time of Paul's visit, tentmaking was very important to Corinth's economy. Two large seaports within a few miles of the city created an ever-present demand for sails. In addition, the biannual Isthmian Games were in progress, requiring tents to house many thousands of spectators. No doubt Paul had no lack of work to provide for his needs.

- Aquila and Priscilla, the tentmakers and believers who had come from Rome, were in exactly the right place at the right time—for their trade and for the establishment of a community of Jesus followers in Corinth. They were established enough to provide work for Paul and had either purchased or rented a shop where they could live, work, and provide a meeting place for a small gathering of Jesus followers. In addition, they had established business contacts in the city and its shops and had met the requirements of the *agoranomos*, the official who controlled commerce in the agora.[25]

- As a tentmaker, Paul put God on display every day. His activities as a businessman—his attitude, integrity, compassion, and fairness to all—helped to show what God and his reign looked like.[26] As Paul worked in the tent shop, likely near the agora, he had a natural opportunity for conversation (and teaching) with his coworkers, customers, nearby merchants, and passersby.

- Leatherwork and tentmaking were physically demanding trades. In the Roman culture, where one's value depended on class and status, manual labor such as tentmaking was looked down upon. But for Paul, the only status that mattered was who he was in Jesus: a redeemed child of God called to the mission of making him known. So Paul humbled himself and imitated Jesus who "was crucified in weakness, yet he lives by God's power."[27] Even though Paul was tired, weak, and inadequate, by God's power he engaged in hard work, toil, and hardship to serve his Lord and Savior.[28]

2. The story of the followers of Jesus in Corinth is much like the story of Israel, and it is important to us because it is our story too. God has a purpose in choosing the least likely of us to be his human partners in restoring *shalom* to his creation. If we, as God's people, will recognize our weakness and depend on him, he will purify us from the chaos of our sin. By his power he will turn our weakness into strength and our inadequacy into a demonstration of his power so that people who do not know him will see

in us the God who loves, redeems, and restores.

Paul clearly describes the weakness, character, and God-given strength of Corinth's Jesus followers. Read the following passages and (1) write down the influence most of them had in Corinth, (2) how Paul described their character before they knew Jesus, and (3) the strength and power God demonstrated through those who served him.

Their influence in the culture	Their quality of character	The source of their strength
1 Corinthians 1:26–28; 7:21–23; 11:22:	1 Corinthians 6:8–11:	1 Corinthians 1:5–7:
		1 Corinthians 1:31:
		1 Corinthians 2:5:
		2 Corinthians 3:4–5:
		2 Corinthians 12:9–10:
		Philippians 4:13:
		Hebrews 11:34:

3. The community of Jesus followers in Corinth was a diverse group representing all social, economic, religious, and racial groups of the melting pot that was Corinth. They stand—as God's people always have—as testimony to the fact that God can and does use anyone to advance his story. God used Moses, a wanted criminal. He used Joseph, a slave, and Israel, a nation of slaves. He used David, the youngest child of his family. He used barren couples, ordinary fishermen, and important public figures. A closer look at some of the believers we know by name provides insight into their diversity and how each contributed to the mission of making God known.

Believer's Name and Description	Source	Their Contribution to the Mission
Priscilla and Aquila: tent-makers from Rome	Acts 18:1–4; 1 Corinthians 16:19	
Titius Justus: God-fearer in the synagogue, likely a Roman citizen	Acts 18:7	
Crispus: synagogue leader, highly respected Jew	Acts 18:8	
Gaius: baptized by Paul	Romans 16:23	
Stephanus and his household (Fortunatus and Achaicus as well)	1 Corinthians 1:16; 16:15–18	
Tertius: a scribe	Romans 16:22	
Erastus: wealthy manager of public facilities—streets, buildings, agora, etc.	Acts 19:22; Romans 16:23; 2 Timothy 4:20	

DID YOU KNOW?
Erastus: A Notable Exception

In 1 Corinthians 1:26, Paul reminded the community of Jesus followers in Corinth that before they knew Jesus and experienced his transforming power in their lives they were for the most part ordinary people—not wise, not influential, and not of noble birth. But we must not overlook notable exceptions. Erastus, for instance, was a Corinthian and trusted coworker of Paul who carried on the work of ministry in Philippi and Thessalonica. Eventually, near the end of Paul's life, Erastus returned to minister in Corinth. The Bible also happens to mention that Erastus was also the city's director of public works.

That may seem like a relatively ordinary occupation to us, but evidence in Corinth tells a different story. In the paved plaza outside the theater entrance, archaeologists found an inscription laid into the floor.

What remains of the inscribed stone pavers reads, "Erastus in return for his *aedileship* laid [missing words] at his own expense." Today we see the inscription cut into the stone, but originally, the letters you see were inlaid with bronze. This inscription gives great recognition and honor to a wealthy and significant person in Corinth.

It appears that the "Erastus" of the inscription is the coworker Paul identifies in Romans 16:23 as the director of public works! "Erastus" is an uncommon name, and when it is linked in both places to the title and position of *aedilis*, or public works director (*oikonomos* in Greek), the connection is quite certain. Apparently, Erastus was very wealthy and important. He was responsible to administer all public facilities including streets, buildings, and the agora, and to collect any revenue those facilities generated. In addition, he carried significant responsibility for the biannual Isthmian Games. In the Roman political system, Erastus would have had to pay a significant sum of money in order to obtain that office and the recognition and benefits it provided.

The wealth and position Erastus had in Corinth would have provided some degree of support and protection for the growing community of believers. His influence likely prevented any opposition from bearing fruit. But most important, his faith in Jesus led him to offer himself as a channel for God's strength and power in order to advance God's kingdom on earth. Even for Erastus, God's power turns weakness into strength. This promise gives God's people the courage and hope to be eager laborers in God's redemption story.

4. Paul began his first letter to the Corinthians with a greeting to "the church of God in Corinth, to those sanctified in Christ Jesus and called to be his holy people."[29] When you hear about a "church" being established in Corinth, what do you imagine it was like? Do you picture a large building where many people gathered to participate in a great worship program, or a small group of people who perhaps met outside like the "place of prayer" Paul described in Philippi, or something altogether different? What do you think church looked like and meant to those who followed Jesus in Corinth as well as in other ancient Roman cities?

What hints does Paul's greeting provide about the true nature and focus of the church in Corinth?

What does the close of Paul's letter to the Corinthians contribute to your understanding of what church was like for the early followers of Jesus? (See 1 Corinthians 16:19–20.)

FOR GREATER UNDERSTANDING
The House Churches of Corinth

We have much to learn from the community of Jesus followers that God's Spirit formed and empowered to be a light that displayed God's character and presence in the Hellenistic culture of Corinth. However, we must be cautious about interpreting that community through the lens of our contemporary church experience. The sign of God's power in Corinth wasn't a mega house church with celebrity-status leadership. Instead, God showed his strength through the weakness of a small, but faithful, community of believers.

In a city of a hundred thousand or more, that community was quite small. Based on Paul's listing of individuals and the extended family households he baptized, a scholarly estimate is about fifty to seventy-five people.[30] Meeting space for a group that size would require a very large villa, so it is generally assumed that the believers in Corinth met in several small house churches located in various parts of the city.

We know Aquila and Priscilla had a tentmaking shop in Corinth and hosted a house church. Permanent shops such as theirs typically were located around the perimeter of the agora or along the streets leading to it. In Corinth, the main agora had fifty shops around the square with a colonnaded portico in front of them that provided a shaded area in front of the shop. The two-story vaulted shops were typically built of stone, about ten to

fifteen feet wide and twelve to twenty-five feet deep, and opened onto the street or agora. The first floor usually was paved in stone and functioned as the workroom for the shopkeeper's trade. About seven feet up, a wooden floor accessed by a ladder created a second story where the shopkeeper's family lived.

The community of Jesus followers would gather in such small, intimate quarters for prayer, worship, praise, teaching, and Holy Communion. In this environment it is easy to see how they, like the first believers, "were together and had everything in common. They sold property and possessions to give to anyone who had need."[31] Paul, Aquila, and Priscilla understood that God's purpose for them was to be a living example of what redemption looks like in every aspect of life. Their business was a means to engage people who did not know God. Their shop and home became a place where new believers met—a Christian synagogue where people shared their lives, were instructed in the Scriptures, and encouraged one another to live in holiness in a very pagan city. This was "church" in Corinth. This was the way God's people became his witnesses to their world.

5. Corinth was known for its temples and shrines—not to the degree Athens was—but the temple of Aphrodite on the Acrocorinth, the temple to Rome and the emperors, and the sanctuary of Poseidon were standouts among many. Each one claimed to house the presence of its respective deity. The more impressive the temple, the more powerful the deity was thought to be. So how could a small community of low-class believers create an impressive display of God's presence in Corinth? The story of how that could happen has everything to do with God's great plan of redemption and the restoration of *shalom* to his beloved creation.[32]

God has always wanted to be present among his people. Through his covenant with Israel, he assured his people of his empowering presence in the ark of the covenant located in the tabernacle and later in his temple in Jerusalem. Then Jesus came to earth and by his death and resurrection restored the intimate relationship between God and his people. Those who encountered Jesus—Immanuel, God with us—experienced the very presence of God among them. On Pentecost, as Jesus' disciples waited, God's presence moved out of the temple in Jerusalem and into a new dwelling place, a new "temple" among the community of those who followed Jesus!

From that day forward, God's people became his house, his temple, the place where his presence dwells. As God's people, empowered by his presence, left Jerusalem and became part of communities of Jesus followers in the most pagan places in their world, God was with them! God's temple—his holy dwelling place on earth—was to be found among the community of his people!

a. How did Paul describe the temple of the Lord in Corinth, and what kind of impact do you think his description had on the community of believers? (See 1 Corinthians 3:16–17.)

DID YOU KNOW?

The Greek word translated as "temple" in 1 Corinthians 3:16–17 is *naos*, and it refers to the inner part of the temple where the god was thought to dwell. So, followers of Jesus are not just part of the temple complex, they are the *naos*—the Holy of Holies in the Hebrew Bible—the place where the very presence of God dwells.

   b. The physical presence of God's temple in Corinth was
       not imposing, but what about that community had an
       amazing power to transform lives? (See 1 John 4:12.)

   c. If the mission of every follower of Jesus is to put God
       on display for the world to see, why does the life of
       the community of God's people matter? (See Ephe-
       sians 2:19–22.)

Reflection

The story of Paul's visit to Corinth is a testimony to God's plan to
use unlikely human partners to accomplish his purpose. By his
grace, God redeems us while we are sinners and commissions
and empowers us to be witnesses who display by our words and
actions what God's *shalom* looks like. That was Paul's mission
and the mission of the Jesus followers in Corinth. Today it is the
mission of every follower of Jesus.

We are God's temple. In the way ancient temples displayed a
god's presence in the world, the community of Christians is to be
a temple that displays God's presence and redeeming power to a
hurting world. As difficult as it is to comprehend why God would
choose flawed human beings to be his temple, that is what we
are! God will provide the strength we need to be his witnesses,
and he will empower our testimony so that people who do not
know God will experience him through us.

The question is, how willing are we to live as God's holy temple, as representatives of his presence in our world?

What does that look like for your life?

All of us to some degree follow our natural tendency to live like the broken world around us. How willing are you to recognize the ways your life shows a broken culture whether or not God's message is valid and take steps to send the right message?

How willing are you to abandon every word and action that assaults God's character and hinders people from knowing the truth about him?

What will it take for you to have the courage to renounce your tendency to serve God in your own strength and boldly take on the "impossible" because God is with you?

THE LORD'S SUPPER: DISCERNING THE BODY

When I walked up the Lechaion Road and into ancient Corinth for the first time, I was deeply moved. Many times I had followed the apostle Paul's dusty footprints through present-day Turkey, and to a lesser extent Greece, each time gaining clearer insight into the Scriptures. But Corinth was different. The connection I felt walking on the same stones Paul had walked seemed stronger and more personal than I had experienced before, and I wasn't sure why.

I thought about how much longer Paul had shared the gospel in this community—nearly two years—than he typically did. Having reread Paul's letters to the Jesus followers of Corinth several times before I visited the city, I was painfully aware of the issues he had tried to resolve within their community. But there was something more. As I began to explore the ruins of Corinth, my thoughts and what I was seeing came into clear focus.

After climbing up the broad stairway where the Lechaion Road opened onto ancient Corinth's sprawling agora, I found myself surrounded by the ruins of a large and impressive city. I looked around, taking in everything I could about the city Paul knew so well. Everywhere I looked—the massive temple of Apollo, the beautiful Peirene fountain, the *bema* in the center of the agora, and the Acrocorinth where the temple of Aphrodite once towered above it all—I saw evidence of Corinth's affluence and religious reputation. Then I saw it. On one side of the agora, across from the *bema*, stood a single vaulted shop.

THE BROAD, PAVED LECHAION ROAD BEGAN AT THE PORT CITY ON THE GULF OF CORINTH AND ENDED AT THE AGORA IN CORINTH. THE PARTIALLY RECONSTRUCTED SHOP BELOW IS TYPICAL OF THE MANY SHOPS THAT LINED THE PERIMETER OF CORINTH'S AGORA.

That small, partially restored shop was like the one where Paul, Aquila, and Priscilla made tents and where the house church met. I stood there for a long time trying to comprehend how large Corinth was and how very small that shop was. Truly the kingdom of heaven came to Corinth like a mustard seed, the smallest of all seeds.[1] By God's grace that small community grew and became a tree that provided shade for many who had wandered, lost in the chaos of the kingdom of this world.

No wonder Paul came to Corinth in weakness, fear, and trembling. His mission was to make God known—not just to win converts but to follow Jesus' instruction to "go and make disciples of all nations . . . teaching them to obey everything I have commanded you."[2] Paul was in Corinth to be a living example of what it means to follow Jesus and to teach—by his every word and action—how to become an example of what life looks like when God is in charge. By the power of God's Spirit, the instruction of the Scriptures, and encouragement in righteousness from one another, that small community of Jesus followers would learn to live as a picture of *shalom* in the midst of a city enmeshed in the chaos of sin.

There's a reason Paul spent more time in Corinth than anywhere else. There's a reason he wrote his longest, most passionate letters to the Jesus followers there. God's people in Corinth came out of great darkness yet they were called to be a light in the darkest places. Paul invited those who would follow Jesus to leave behind their cultural lifestyle, the path of chaos, and join God's way of *shalom*. It wasn't easy. In the same way Moses discovered that it was easier to get Israel out of Egypt than it was to get "Egypt" out of Israel, Paul came to the realization that it wasn't easy to get "Corinth" out of the new Corinthian believers.

The community of believers in Corinth grew quickly, but they encountered many obstacles on the way to becoming God's kingdom of priests, a holy temple that displayed his presence to the world. They found it difficult to leave behind the ethical, moral, and social practices of their former pagan lifestyle. Paul encountered some of his greatest victories and toughest challenges as he offered instruction and correction to this community of Jesus followers about how to live in the love and unity needed to display God's true character and establish his kingdom in Corinth.

That small shop in Corinth stands out in my mind as a visual testimony to the Holy Spirit's transforming power. As I walked out of the agora, I felt renewed, encouraged, and hopeful for those of us who follow Jesus in our world. Like that little house church in Corinth, we live in a deeply divided and self-focused world. The cultural conflicts and struggles they faced are just as real for us as they were for them. If we become more like that small, faithful community and *together*—as a community of God's redeemed people who share in the most important mission in all of God's creation—show our world what *shalom* looks like, we can have a transforming influence on our world too.

Opening Thoughts (3 minutes)

The Very Words of God

> *I appeal to you, brothers and sisters, in the name of our Lord Jesus Christ, that all of you agree with one another in what you say and that there be no divisions among you, but that you be perfectly united in mind and thought.*
>
> **1 Corinthians 1:10**

Think About It

Many people in our culture like to think of themselves as progressive, inclusive, and unfettered by "outdated" traditions and values. But if we look closely, our culture is much like the Hellenistic culture of ancient Corinth. In the Roman Empire, economic, social, and political status (and the security, respect, and power associated with one's status) was rigidly defined. Everyone knew who the winners were, and the vast majority of people were losers, forced to view the "good life" from the outside. Although our cultural definitions of winners and losers are subject to change and some people can better their status, the great divide between winners and losers remains evident in every aspect of life.

Which economic, social, political, or other examples of one's status do you think define and divide winners and losers in our culture? Money, Class, Fame

What do Jesus followers today have to offer people who our culture defines as "losers," people who are cast to the outside of a meaningful life and feel alienated and desperate to be respected, accepted, and loved? *Jesus*

Video Notes (33 minutes)

The Father's house: a different social order

Who is Lord?

The message of a Roman city

The message of tassels

Paul's message for Corinth

Paul meets a community of believers in Corinth

Living as God's community in a Roman world

    Class means everything

    A banquet in the Dolphin house

Paul's countercultural message: we are one in Christ!

The Lord's Supper

Visible proof that the gospel is real

Video Discussion (6 minutes)

1. Paul walked into Corinth to fulfill the mission Jesus gave
   to him: to make God known to the Jews first, then to the
   Gentiles. He knew he was called to be a light to the Gentiles. He knew he was part of God's kingdom of priests
   being built up as a suitable temple where God's presence
   would live among them.

   a. How excited and encouraged do you think Paul was
      when he learned there was already a community of
      Jesus followers in Corinth, and why would this have
      made a difference to him?

   b. What did you think when you saw the type of house
      where the "church," the community of believers in
      Corinth, would have gathered for worship? In what
      ways was it different from the elegant gatherings in
      the "dolphin" house on Delos where people no doubt
      were seated and served according to their status?

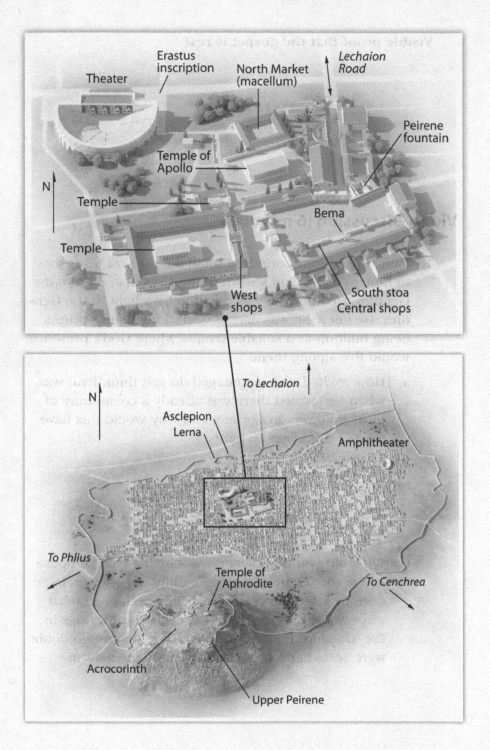

Theater

Erastus inscription

North Market (macellum)

Lechaion Road

Peirene fountain

Temple of Apollo

N

Temple

Bema

Temple

West shops

South stoa

Central shops

To Lechaion

N

Asclepion

Lerna

Amphitheater

To Phlius

Temple of Aphrodite

To Cenchrea

Acrocorinth

Upper Peirene

2. When Paul walked into the Roman colony of Corinth, he
    witnessed the result of close to a hundred years of sig-
    nificant infrastructure development (paid for by Rome)
    that had transformed it into a large and prosperous city.
    On the map of Corinth, note the location of the agora
    and the major temples as well as the roads to Lechaion
    and Cenchrea, the seaport towns that had contributed so
    much to the city's wealth and reputation.

3. As you watched the video, what did you realize about the
    way Hellenism and the social order of the Roman world
    dictated everyday life in Corinth?

    In what ways does this understanding help you to better
    understand the meaning and passion of Paul's concern
    about how the followers of Jesus in Corinth lived and
    thereby showed what God is like?

    Why was it important to him that the Corinthian believers
    be "one body"—to be and live like a loving community?

4. Even though Paul came to Corinth in what he described
   as weakness, fear, and trembling, he seems tireless in
   sharing God's message—teaching as well as demonstrating what life looks like when God's kingdom reigns. He
   repeatedly critiques (but doesn't criticize) the Roman values and way of life by advocating and demonstrating the
   opposing values of God's kingdom. Which of his teachings that contrast the values of God's kingdom to those of
   Rome made the greatest impression on you, and why?

Which values of our culture do you think the gospel message turns upside down?

To what extent do you think Jesus followers today are
committed to living out the "upside down" values of the
gospel every day, and what are the consequences of our
commitment to the mission God has given us?

Small Group Bible Discovery and Discussion (14 minutes)

Paul Calls God's Family to Live in Harmony

God has always intended for the community of his redeemed people to live in obedience to his commands so that they will be living witnesses of his character and show the *shalom* that is possible when life is lived in obedience to his will. God made this clear at Mount Sinai when he set apart the Hebrew people—Israel—to be his holy nation and kingdom of priests. He commissioned them to obey his commands fully so that they would create a unique culture—a culture of righteousness—and stand out as a distinct people among the pagan cultures around them. He wanted them, as a committed and unified community, to put his character on display and show what every activity of life looks like when his kingdom reigns.

In a similar way, Paul called the communities of Jesus followers in Corinth to be living models of the culture of God's kingdom. Their uniqueness was not so much in the visual sense of dress, diet, language, or architecture that we often view as cultural distinctions, but in the sense of being living witnesses of the nature of God's character and showing through their lifestyle and relationships what living in the kingdom of heaven looks like. Paul challenged them to live as a little colony of heaven planted in the midst of Corinth.

The Corinthians understood this concept very well because at the time Corinth (like Philippi) was a Roman colony. Life in Corinth, then, was lived according to the practices, laws, and customs of Rome and provided a real taste of what it would be like to live in Rome. In the same way, the life of God's people was to provide a taste of what it would be like to live in heaven. The moral purity, righteousness, ethics, compassion, generosity, integrity, and concern for others that was woven into the fabric of daily life of the community of Jesus defined their culture and set them apart from the Hellenistic culture of Corinth and the Roman Empire.

For this reason, the community of Jesus followers had to leave behind the pagan culture of their former lives and fully embrace the culture of righteousness. The very small house church communities were God's priesthood in Corinth, bearing the very presence of God among people who were alienated from him. They were to be examples of what life in the kingdom of heaven looks like—a picture of *shalom* restored to a broken world. They made God known and demonstrated his character and will by their words and the testimony of their lives. Righteousness lived out in everyday life was crucial to their mission because it made their witness both faithful and credible.

Paul was very concerned that the community of Jesus followers in Corinth radically demonstrate the "culture" of God's *shalom*. So his instructions to the community often related to the importance of holy living and unity. If any members of the believing community fell back into the lifestyle of the kingdom of this world, it would seriously undermine their mission. Furthermore, as a small community charged with the mission of making God known in a large city, it was essential that there be no division or dissension: they must be one "body," the body of Jesus the Messiah.

DID YOU KNOW?
The Culture of a Holy Nation
At Mount Sinai, God set apart the Hebrew people as his own to stand out as a unique, holy nation among the pagan cultures that lived around them. So that Israel would know how to live as his holy nation, God gave them specific commands related to purity, identity, relationships, dress, diet, health, worship, and social practices. In addition to setting them apart in their lifestyle, relationships, and worship, God commanded specific outward symbols of their identity. One of those commands was to wear tassels (Hebrew, *tzitzit*) on their clothing as a constant reminder to obey God's commands always and to live in the world as his kingdom of priests.[3]

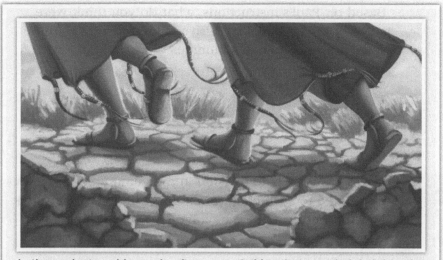

In the ancient world, people often wore clothing that revealed their identity and social status. The hem and tassels of the outer robe typically symbolized the owner's identity and authority. People in the upper classes, for example—nobility, kings, and princes—decorated their hems with tassels. So the tassels God commanded his people to wear gave them a clear and distinct identity. Everyone who saw them would recognize who they were. Furthermore, the tassels included a blue cord the color of the priests' garments that served to remind both Jews and Gentiles of the Jews' status as God's holy, chosen people.[4]

1. What is Paul's clear message about unity in the community of Jesus followers, and why would he emphasize it in his instruction to people in the highly class-conscious culture of the Roman Empire? (See 1 Corinthians 12:12–13; Galatians 3:26–28.)

Based on Paul's instructions, what do you think were some of the potentially divisive cultural conflicts in the small house church communities of Corinth?

Envy

In what ways would division in the community of believers related to such conflicts diminish the mission of making God known and being a light to the Gentiles?

2. In the strict class system of the Roman Empire, no one from the emperor down to the lowest galley slave could imagine a culture like the one Paul advocated for the community of Jesus followers. (See Philippians 2:1–11.)

   a. Which qualities of character and relationships did Paul consider to be necessary in the community of those who are redeemed and united in Christ?

   b. Who did Paul lift up as the person who exemplifies these values of the kingdom of heaven?

c.	In what way does a life that exemplifies such a culture fulfill the mission God has given to those who follow him?

FOR GREATER UNDERSTANDING
The Culture of the Father's House

If we are to grasp the meaning of the biblical concept of being restored to God's family, we need to understand the central role the extended family played in ancient Middle Eastern culture. The extended family, or household as it was sometimes called, was considered to be "the father's house," or *beth ab* in Hebrew. Such a household could easily comprise thirty or more family members from several generations: the head of the family (the patriarch), his wife (or wives), his younger brothers, unmarried children, and married sons with their families (a woman usually joined the *beth ab* of her husband).

The job of the patriarch was to use the family resources, which he controlled, to ensure the protection and care of each family member. Yes, the patriarch held a powerful position in the extended family, but that position existed for the benefit and care of the family and its individual members. If a family member lost connection to the *beth ab* due to capture by enemies, poverty, or bad choices, the patriarch was responsible to do whatever it took, to make whatever sacrifices were necessary, in order to restore that person to the safety and fellowship of the family. Anyone in that cultural setting who lost the support or protection of the *beth ab*, such as a widow or orphan, faced serious risk.

We need to have the image of the *beth ab* in mind when we read about God's longing to redeem and restore every one of his children who has been lost due to bondage to sin. God is the loving Father who longs to embrace his children in the security and blessing of his *beth ab*. And, as Abraham realized thousands of years ago, God wants his human partners to join him in the mission of putting him on display so that those who are estranged from him—even his most broken, lost, and hopeless children—can experience restoration and faithful care in the *beth ab*.

Imagine, if you will, how countercultural the social order of the *beth ab* would be in Corinth. Imagine the impact a community of Jesus followers would have if they lived like a *beth ab* in a city where the Hellenistic, Roman perspective of distinct and self-serving classes dominated the culture and affected every aspect of daily life. Imagine a community of believers seeking out and welcoming into their fellowship every individual their heavenly Father redeemed and restored from the kingdom of the Evil One. Imagine the forgiveness, mutual support, and unity that could be possible in God's family if only they would obey him.

3. First Peter 2:4–5 describes those who have chosen to follow Jesus and joined God's kingdom as "being built into a spiritual house to be a holy priesthood." The term "spiritual house" refers to a temple, and the priesthood represents and makes known the God of the temple. Paul uses the same familiar cultural metaphor to describe God's people in order to teach followers of Jesus how to live as a community. (See 1 Corinthians 3:16–17; 2 Corinthians 6:16; Ephesians 2:19–22.)

   a. What do you learn from these passages about the close, family-like, holy nature of the community?

b. Just as the stones of ancient temples were carefully worked to fit together perfectly, the community of believers are living stones that are carefully fit together to build God's temple. What happens to a building if the individual stones are in conflict, and what happens to the temple that is intended to display God's presence in the world if its individual members are in conflict?

c. How important is it for the community of God's people to recognize their unity and their role in being *built together* into God's temple—his holy dwelling place?

d. What impact do you think the unity of that community (or lack thereof) would have on their mission, and why?

Faith Lesson (3 minutes)

The gospel has always attracted people who struggle with life's challenges, whether those struggles be hunger, loneliness, disease, oppression, the emptiness of a life without purpose or meaning, or the despair of being trapped in a class system they cannot escape. A significant portion of the early community of Jesus followers comprised the poor, the slaves, and the marginalized. It was no different in Corinth. Many who lived in the cultural chaos of that pagan city received the good news eagerly.

Those who accepted the truth of Paul's message were welcomed into the community of Jesus followers. There, where the presence of God reigned in the hearts and lives of his people, they were accepted, loved, cared for, and treated with dignity no matter what their status. There was no slave or free, no rich or poor, no Jew or Gentile. All were one in Jesus and shared with one another as each had a need. As they demonstrated God's *shalom* in their daily lives and in their relationships as a community of believers, others were drawn to join this radically different movement.

Stone by stone, a new temple was being built in Corinth! Structurally and visually it was not as dramatic as the temples of Aphrodite, Poseidon, Ascelepius, or the Roman emperors. Its physical presence was not as imposing, but its power to transform lives was amazing. In the simple homes and shops of Stephanas, Priscilla and Aquila, and others, the very presence of God lived and showed to those in chaos the loving compassion of the Creator. The holiness and unity of their lives mattered because they were witnesses of the true God and his kingdom.

1. In Corinth, people saw in the community of believers the presence of God. That presence became real to them through the love, generosity, and compassion of God's people. In that presence many of them found forgiveness and restoration to their Creator.

    What specific things do you think demonstrate the character and presence of God to people in our culture?

    Love,
    Compassion,

How unified, intentional, and authentic do you think the Christian community—God's temple in our world—is in demonstrating God's presence in these ways?

What specific things might we do better individually and as a community?

2. What difference does it make to the mission of making God known when righteousness, love, compassion, and acceptance are lived out by only an individual or two in contrast to being the normal behavior of an entire community of Jesus followers?

3. Why do you think a community that lives in harmony and unity is so important to the mission of making God known?

Closing (1 minute)

Read 1 John 3:16–18 aloud together: "This is how we know what love is: Jesus Christ laid down his life for us. And we ought to lay down our lives for our brothers and sisters. If anyone has material possessions and sees a brother or sister in need but has no pity on them, how can the love of God be in that person? Dear children, let us not love with words or speech but with actions and in truth."

Then pray, thanking God for his great love shown to all of humankind through the death and resurrection of his son, Jesus. Ask for a heart like the selfless heart of Jesus that gladly lays aside pride, status, comfort, and material possessions for the benefit of others. Pray that God's love will overflow our hearts as we become willing servants and living examples who demonstrate his love and character through our every word and action. Ask God to make us, as a community of his partners, like a colony of heaven that shows what God's *shalom*—life lived on earth as it is in heaven—looks like in a dark and hurting world. Pray that our lives will encourage our brothers and sisters in Christ as we faithfully pursue the mission together. Ask God to anoint our words and deeds so that his lost children see in us a true and faithful testimony of the Holy Spirit's transforming power and will want to experience that transformation in their hearts and lives.

Memorize

This is how we know what love is: Jesus Christ laid down his life for us. And we ought to lay down our lives for our brothers and sisters. If anyone has material possessions and sees a brother or sister in need but has no pity on them, how can the love of God be in that person? Dear children, let us not love with words or speech but with actions and in truth.

1 John 3:16–18

Making God Known in a Broken World

In-Depth Personal Study Sessions

Study 1 | Presenting Biblical Truth in the Language of the Culture

The Very Words of God

> Though I am free and belong to no one, I have made myself a slave to everyone, to win as many as possible. To the Jews I became like a Jew, to win the Jews. To those under the law I became like one under the law (though I myself am not under the law), so as to win those under the law. To those not having the law I became like one not having the law (though I am not free from God's law but am under Christ's law), so as to win those not having the law. To the weak I became weak, to win the weak. I have become all things to all people so that by all possible means I might save some. I do all this for the sake of the gospel, that I may share in its blessings.
>
> **1 Corinthians 9:19–23**

Bible Discovery

Paul Teaches Through the Metaphors of Life in Corinth

A person doesn't have to read much of the Bible to recognize the unique way its ancient Jewish writers often communicated theological truth through metaphors, stories, and word pictures. God is shepherd, living water, husband, and father. His people are his flock, servants, bride, and children. Jesus is the bread of life, true vine, Lamb, King, door, gate, and light. The more a person knows about the setting of God's inspired story and the mindset of the people to whom it was written, the more vibrant and meaningful these descriptions of deep theological truth become.

In contrast, people immersed in Western culture prefer to understand biblical truth in terms of proposition or systematic explanation. This mindset is preferred not only by contemporary Christians in the West, but was preferred by the first-century Greek world as well. I have heard someone describe the difference in communication as the Hebrew prefers an illustration while the Greek prefers a concept. This is why the book of Isaiah, for example, reads quite differently from the book of Romans. Isaiah was written for a Jewish audience with a traditional Eastern mindset; Romans was written for a Greek audience with a Western mindset (meaning culturally Greek or Western, not exclusively Greek geographically). It is important to realize that the truth of the Bible doesn't change even though theological truth can be expressed in different ways so that it is meaningful to people of different cultures.

It is striking to discover how well the early disciples of Jesus who were raised and trained, for the most part, in the Eastern mindset of traditional Jewish culture understood the pagan culture of their world and communicated the gospel message using its language and metaphors. Paul, for example, was a master at using the traditional Hebrew practice of expressing the truth of Scripture through cultural metaphors and word pictures—just as the writers of the Hebrew Text and Jesus had done with great skill and impact. However, when communicating to Gentiles who understood their world through a Greek or Western mindset, Paul used metaphors and word pictures in a significantly different way. He still used the Hebrew Text as the source of his teaching, but he expressed its truth using the familiar cultural metaphors of the Greco-Roman world in which his audience lived. We see this clearly in his letters to the early churches. His letters to Corinth are a testimony to his rabbinic training and how well he knew his audience. Let's consider some of the metaphors he used and the biblical truth they present.

1. Agriculture was an important part of Corinth's economy. For centuries, rich topsoil washed down from the hillsides surrounding Corinth and produced fertile soil for vineyards and other fruit and vegetables. People passed through these vineyards and fields when entering the city, so they were familiar with the agriculture in the area. Read each of the following passages and write in your own words how Paul used agricultural metaphors to communicate what the Scriptures teach about living according to the culture of God's kingdom as opposed to the pagan culture of Corinth.

    a. 1 Corinthians 3:4–9: the seed, those who plant, those who water, the one who makes things grow, the field

    b. 1 Corinthians 9:7–11: reward for one who plants a vineyard, reward for one who tends a flock, the ox that treads the grain, the hope of harvest for whoever plows and threshes

    c. 2 Corinthians 9:6–11: sowing and reaping sparingly vs. sowing and reaping generously, the one who supplies seed, bread, the increase and harvest

2. During the first century AD, the Olympic Games were wildly popular in the Roman Empire. People flocked to see the star performers compete in honor of the gods and the emperors. Like today, Olympic athletes were heroes. The second most popular games in the Roman Empire were the biannual Isthmian Games. Dedicated to Poseidon, god of the sea, events were held in a stadium, theater, and hippodrome complex near the temple of Poseidon not far from Corinth. Competitors in field events such as discus, javelin, foot races, and long jump; wrestling; boxing; chariot racing; poetry; and music vied for one prize only. There were no "silver" or "bronze" winners. Read 1 Corinthians 9:19–27 and consider how Paul used metaphors from the games to communicate what the Scriptures teach about living according to the culture of God's kingdom.

    a. What is Paul willing to do to "win," and what prize does he want so badly? (See 1 Corinthians 9:19–23.)

b. In order to participate in the Isthmian Games, athletes committed to train for ten months in preparation for the competition. The discipline of their training also required an oath to the god Poseidon that they would abstain from wine, meat, and sexual intercourse during that ten-month period of time! (See 1 Corinthians 9:24–25.)

Which metaphors does Paul use to convey that the life of a Jesus follower is not a spectator activity but a fierce contest that requires utmost dedication, discipline, and perseverance?

How effective and motivational do you think these images would have been to his audience? To people today?

c. Which strong, visual images does Paul use to convey the intent and purpose of his training and vigorous fight for the gospel? (See 1 Corinthians 9:26–27.)

3. In 146 BC, during the expansion of the Roman Empire, Corinth was totally destroyed. It remained nothing more than a small village until 44 BC when Julius Caesar designated it a Roman colony and began a program to restore its wealth and prestige. When Paul arrived in Corinth in 50 AD, he would have seen the results of a massive urban renewal program that the Roman emperors had been financing for about one hundred years. So construction was a familiar sight to residents of Corinth that provided rich metaphors for Paul to use in describing the community of Jesus followers (the house churches) that was being built in Corinth. (See 1 Corinthians 3:10–17.)

   a. What is the foundation of what God was building in Corinth, and what was Paul's role in it?

   b. Which images does Paul use to describe the importance and value of what is being built on that foundation?

      How effectively do you think these images convey the value and risk associated with each believer's contribution to God's work in building a colony of heaven in Corinth?

What do these images lead you to think about regarding your own contribution to the spread of God's kingdom in your everyday world?

c. What do Paul's metaphors communicate about how important it is to build up rather than tear down what God is building, and how effective would you say they are in inspiring believers to diligently pursue the mission today?

4. Corinth was famous for the manufacture of bronze implements and decorative items such as statues. These items were valuable because of the intrinsic worth of the metal and the beauty of items made from it.[5] Corinthian bronze had a distinctive color and could be polished to a very high sheen, so one of its uses was to make mirrors. Corinthian bronze provided a unique metaphor through which Paul could convey important insight into a believer's walk with God.

a. To help project sound to the audience in a theater, a large bronze vase would be placed below the stage. Although that large, vibrating vessel helped people hear the actors' voices, the clarity of their words was muffled. Using this metaphor, what was Paul's message about proclaiming the gospel without love? (See 1 Corinthians 13:1.)

b. Bronze mirrors produced dim reflections, unlike the bright, clear images of glass mirrors today. How did this well-known quality of bronze mirrors help Paul to convey the importance of humility and encourage growth and maturity in a believer's walk with God? (See 1 Corinthians 13:12; 2 Corinthians 3:18.)

5. Corinthian pottery was a highly desired treasure among the upper classes of Roman society. The famous vases painted with figures in black, red, and white were exported throughout the Mediterranean world. Paul likely had this type of pottery in mind in his encouragement to the community of believers in 2 Corinthians 4:6–9. Notice how skillfully Paul created a contrast to this image of value in order to make a powerful statement about the true value of those who follow Jesus faithfully.

a. We naturally expect a precious treasure to be contained in a valuable vessel—the more exotic the treasure, the more exquisite its container. In contrast, what treasure does Paul say those who follow Jesus have in ordinary clay jars—jars that are used for the most mundane tasks of daily life and over time crack, break, and crumble?

b. In terms of understanding what is truly valuable in life and worthy of recognition in people, what do you think Paul wanted his readers to realize about what appears to be "fancy pottery" and what appears to be "clay jars"?

c. In what ways do you think this image would have encouraged each and every believer in the small house churches of Corinth?

Reflection

Paul's first disciple, Timothy,[6] became like a beloved son to him. The two men labored side-by-side to make the gospel message known and to establish churches in cities such as Berea, Corinth, and Ephesus. They were in Corinth during the Isthmian Games, and Paul uses familiar images of athletic training and competition in letters he later wrote to encourage Timothy in the difficult work he had sent him to accomplish in Ephesus.

Read the following passages of personal concern and advice that Paul wrote to Timothy as his mentor, co-laborer in the gospel, and friend. Then consider each passage as Paul's wisdom and advice to you in your walk with God.

1 Timothy 4:7–10: "Have nothing to do with godless myths and old wives' tales; rather, train yourself to be godly. For physical training is of some value, but godliness has value for all things, holding promise for both the present life and the life to come. This is a trustworthy saying that deserves full acceptance. That is why we labor and strive, because we have put our hope in the living God, who is the Savior of all people, and especially of those who believe."

What does training—physical or spiritual—provide for us when we face intense challenges in everyday life and ministry?

Why do we labor in God's kingdom, and how much and what kind of training do we need for this work?

2 Timothy 2:1, 5: "You then, my son, be strong in the grace that is in Christ Jesus . . . anyone who competes as an athlete does not receive the victor's crown except by competing according to the rules."
In the Isthmian Games, all athletes swore an oath to Poseidon that they would follow the rules of the competition. What are the "rules" for finishing strong as followers of Jesus, and how do they help us represent him well?

What happens when we try to follow Jesus according to our own rules?

2 Timothy 4:6–8: "For I am already being poured out like a drink offering, and the time for my departure is near. I have fought the good fight, I have finished the race, I have kept the faith. Now there is in store for me the crown of righteousness, which the Lord, the righteous Judge, will award to me on that day—and not only to me, but also to all who have longed for his appearing."

What do you realize from this passage about the way Paul approached his "walk" with Jesus?

What challenge and encouragement do you think Timothy received by Paul's testimony of how he ran the race God had laid out for him?

How do you want to finish the race God has set out for you?

How intensely will you train, discipline yourself, and compete for your crown of righteousness?

Study 2 | Cultural Conflict within the House Church Communities

The Very Words of God

> Brothers and sisters, I could not address you as people who live by the
> Spirit but as people who are still worldly—mere infants in Christ. . . .
> For since there is jealousy and quarreling among you, are you not
> worldly? Are you not acting like mere humans?

1 Corinthians 3:1, 3

Bible Discovery

Learning to Live by the Cultural Values of God's Kingdom

Wherever he went, Paul shared the good news of the kingdom of
heaven, and the kingdom of this world was not pleased. In fact,
Paul's message always stirred up conflict, which should not surprise anyone who has studied Scripture. The Bible teaches that
there have always been two kingdoms, each advocating a worldview that shapes the values, norms, and social behavior of its
unique culture. One kingdom embraces the worldview of the Evil
One and elevates the desires of the human person as the central
focus in life. The other kingdom recognizes a worldview where
God is Lord and King and the greatest privilege in life is to obey
all that he commands. Since the day our human ancestors chose
the enticement of the Evil One over obedience to the commands
God gave them, the conflict between these two kingdoms has
played out through human history.

Sometimes the clash literally results in conflict between God's
people and the people around them. Paul's message, for instance,
was not a challenge to any political system, but the claims of
God's kingdom implied ethical, moral, religious, and economic
values that clearly clashed with the dominant political kingdom
of the day: the Roman Empire. This resulted in life-threatening
opposition in Philippi, Thessalonica, and Berea. In Athens
and Corinth, where the glory of the ancient Greeks had been
absorbed into the Roman Empire, the same political issues did

not result in overt, life-threatening conflict. This does not mean, however, that there was no conflict between God's kingdom and the kingdom of this world in Corinth.

Quite the opposite was true. The conflict wasn't about politics, but it was real. The challenge Paul's message presented in Corinth resulted in a cultural clash played out as much within the house church communities as in the interaction between followers of Jesus and those who did not yet believe the good news. Some Jesus followers were faithful to their calling while others were still influenced by the culture of their life before they knew Jesus, so discord and a lack of unity diminished their testimony for the gospel.

As Jesus showed his followers when he bound "the strong man,"[7] God's transforming power at work in the hearts of people who follow Jesus as their Lord and King can take back the territory the Evil One has stolen from God and thereby extend God's reign on earth. Fighting to take back lives for the kingdom of God is at the heart of Paul's ministry in Corinth. But the Evil One does not relinquish one square inch of his kingdom without a struggle, and the struggle for the hearts of the Corinthians led to cultural conflict both outside and within the house church communities.

Paul passionately addressed that clash of cultures through extensive teaching on the purity of heart and lifestyle that God intended the "culture" of his redeemed people to demonstrate. They could no longer live by the cultural norms of the kingdom from which they had been redeemed. This is why Paul taught about such big cultural issues as appropriate social and spiritual behavior and love and unity in the body of Christ.

1. After Paul left Corinth to minister in Ephesus, the community of Jesus followers in Corinth struggled to continue growing in godliness. It seems the culture of their pagan past began shaping the culture of God's people. Some of the believers were no longer living in a way that put God's character on display and demonstrated the *shalom* of what life looks like when God's kingdom reigns.

The community had divided according to the values and norms of the pagan culture rather than being unified as God's holy temple and loving *beth ab*.

a. Which issues rooted in the pagan culture of Corinth apparently had become divisive and destructive to the community of God's people and their message? (See 1 Corinthians 5:1; 6:1; 7:1; 8:1; 10:14; 11:17–22; 12:1; 16:1–3.)

b. On what basis did Paul appeal to the believers in Corinth to change their ways? (See 1 Corinthians 1:2–3, 9–10.)

DID YOU KNOW?
Opposing Cultures in Corinth

The culture of the Roman Empire as it was lived in Corinth focused on a person's status, which determined one's significance. Elaborate expressions of one's status, such as hosting banquets for important guests, were encouraged. Empathy and compassion for others, especially those who were of a lower class, were discouraged. One's own status was far more important than that of another.

In contrast, the mission of God's people always has been to display a radically different culture from that of pagan people so that they can see what *shalom* looks like. So God instructed his people to live in harmony and unity. Continuing this instruction, Jesus taught his disciples that their unity and love for each other would prove the truth of their message to people around them. Paul also taught the house church communities about the importance of their unity and love by using the images of each person being a stone built into one temple where God's Spirit lived and each person being one member of one body joined together in fellowship and service to God.

Above all, Jesus modeled a culture of love and empathy extended to all people, even the oppressed and those society viewed as worthless. Jesus taught his disciples to imitate him in their love for one another and their concern for those who were poor, hungry, thirsty, lonely, sick, or in prison. He went so far as to command his followers to love their neighbors and their enemies. Unlike the self-serving culture of Corinth, the culture of God's kingdom bestows honor to those who demonstrate the selfless love of Jesus.

2. Every culture has unique perspectives, a hierarchy of values, and certain acceptable behaviors. After leaving Corinth, Paul received news from the believers he left behind that showed the values of Corinth's pagan culture were gaining influence in his beloved church communities. Some members were focused more on promoting their own status at the expense of others than they were on advancing God's reign in their city. In an effort to clearly define and establish an appropriate culture for the community of God's people in Corinth, Paul responded using passionate words of correction and wisdom. (See 1 Corinthians 1:10–31; 3:1–9.)

    a. Which cultural contrasts in perspective, thought, status, and behavior does Paul highlight in these passages? List as many as you can!

b. Did Paul consider jealousy, quarrels, and boasting
    to be characteristic of Corinth's pagan culture or the
    culture of God's kingdom, and what did he want the
    believers to realize about such behavior?

c. Which examples of the way God turns our human
    values upside down stand out to you, and how do the
    contrasts Paul highlights help us to recognize our true
    status in God's kingdom?

3. Roman culture was built on taking action to protect
    and enhance whatever may be in "my" best interest and
    increase "my" status, regardless of the impact on others.
    Which opposing priorities does Paul present as appropri-
    ate for the culture of the house church? (See 1 Corinthi-
    ans 10:23–24, 31–33.)

What does Paul teach is the intent of a believer's every
action, and in what ways does this purpose define the
culture of the house church?

Why is it important for every believer to respect the struggles of weaker believers? (See 1 Corinthians 8:9–13.)

How different from their "natural" way of living would it be for Jesus followers in Corinth to make lifestyle choices that served the best interest of others rather than themselves?

FOR GREATER UNDERSTANDING
Class and Status in the Roman Empire

Social class divided the Roman world, including Corinth. Unlike today, where class and status are somewhat dynamic, allowing people to gain higher economic status and to interact with people of differing status, the Roman class hierarchy was very rigid. There was no sense of equality that superseded class status; movement to a higher class was not possible; and there was no intermarriage between classes. Although some slaves could gain their freedom, a person could expect to remain in the class he or she was born into for life.

The class system was deeply rooted in every aspect of life in the Roman Empire. As such, it became a significant obstacle to the love, respect, mutual honor, and unity God desired the house church communities to exemplify in Corinth.

- Roman Emperor—the top of the Roman class system.

- Senator—this class included a few hundred families, nearly all in Italy, that owned property worth at least one million sesterces, which had an approximate value of several million U.S. dollars.[8]

- Equestrian—originally comprised those who served in the military and were wealthy enough to pay for their horse, weapons, and support (through plunder of a defeated enemy). Only a few thousand in the empire owned property equal to 400,000 sesterces and had the moral excellence approved by the Roman Senate to qualify for this status.

- Decurion—this was a much larger class of elite aristocrats and government officials, many of whom became wealthy by taking advantage of their positions. Qualifications for this status included property worth at least 100,000 sesterces and senatorial approval. Members of this class often showed off their wealth by hosting elaborate and decadent banquets.

- Middle Class—sometimes called the "respectable populace." These were landowners, shopkeepers, and craftsmen, including former slaves who had acquired their freedom. Their status was evident by the number of slaves or hired help who did their work. They occasionally held banquets like the upper classes or participated in trade guild feasts. As tentmakers, Paul, Aquila, and Priscilla may have belonged to this class.

- The Poor—including freed slaves or freeborn, this group may have accounted for one-third of the population of the Roman Empire. Many were former landowners who had lost their farms due to unpaid debts. They generally lived at a subsistence level, sometimes working for the wealthier person to whom they had lost their land or finding other work in service to a wealthy family. Many of the poor congregated in the cities and in Rome grew to such a large number that they received a daily subsidy of grain in order to help maintain the peace.

- The Slaves—were considered to be inferior and were viewed as property, not as humans with dignity and innate value. Because of Corinth's prosperity and location as one of the empire's largest slave markets, the city likely had a significant slave population.

4. The Corinthian's drive to promote one's personal status was so pervasive that even the exercise of their spiritual gifts became competitive and divisive. What did Paul teach about the source, purpose, and benefit of spiritual gifts in order to show the "better way" of God's kingdom as opposed to the self-serving culture of the believers' pagan past? (See 1 Corinthians 12:1–11.)

    Read 1 Corinthians 13:1–7 as if you were a follower of Jesus who had known no other culture than the self-serving culture of Corinth. In what ways would Paul's teaching about the "better way" of love be a contrast to how you lived life, and how would it help you to understand how to live life in God's community?

5. Roman society was litigious, and the process of seeking justice was corrupted by rampant bribery. Even so, some believers were suing other believers in Roman courts. (See 1 Corinthians 6:1–11.)

    a. For which reasons did such activity within the community of faith offend Paul?

    b. What did such behavior reveal about the believers' attachment to the way of life they knew before they were "washed . . . sanctified . . . justified" in the name of Jesus?

c. What kinds of selfless—even counterintuitive—
behavior does Paul present as appropriate options for
dealing with conflict in the culture of God's kingdom?

6. Which behavior—that was even unlawful by pagan cultural standards—did the Corinthian house churches tolerate? (See 1 Corinthians 5:1–8.)

What impact would such behavior have on the community of Jesus followers and on their mission as representatives of God's kingdom on earth? (See Leviticus 18:24–27.)

PROFILE OF A CULTURE
A Place at the Banquet

The upper classes of Roman society displayed their wealth and status by making public donations, wearing expensive clothing that was illegal for the lower classes, acquiring more and higher quality slaves, and increasing their entourage of clients. They also displayed their wealth and status by hosting banquets, called *deipnon*, to celebrate virtually every religious, civic, or personal occasion.[9] These banquets were held in private homes as well as in temple banquet halls.

The wealthiest individuals lived in large villas with a central columned courtyard open to the sky, elaborate frescoes on the walls, and beautiful mosaic floors. These homes typically included a large banquet room for entertaining the most important guests, plus other rooms where less important guests would be served—all in order according to their status.

A VILLA ON THE ISLAND OF DELOS IS TYPICAL OF THE HOMES IN WHICH THE WEALTHY WOULD ENTERTAIN THEIR GUESTS.

The host sat at one end of the dining room, or *triclinium*, in which low couches were arranged in a horseshoe shape so that guests could recline on their left arm to eat with their right hand. The guests of highest honor sat on the host's right and left, and the remaining guests filled in other places in descending order of their class. The lowest class guests were seated farthest from the host, sometimes in separate rooms, and the poor were left outside.

When the food was served, the highest status guests received the finest food and drink before anyone else. The remaining food was served according to class, with the poor eating last if at all. A *symposion*, or drinking party, where wine was consumed to excess, followed the food service. Entertainment during the *symposion* might include musical performance, philosophical discourse, juggling, or acrobatics. It also included a wide variety of sexual entertainment provided by trained female companions, *hetaerae*, as well as by slaves and boys.

These cultural banquets were the setting in which the Corinthians declared and enhanced their social status. Such banquets were a common practice. Given this background, it is easier to understand why it was a struggle to keep division and immorality from destroying the house church communities and the testimony of God's people.

Reflection

The Hellenistic philosophy of the ancient Greeks provided the worldview on which the Corinthians based their cultural values. Their belief system elevated the human being as the focal point of the universe. The ultimate goal in life, then, was to satisfy one's desires for happiness, pleasure, power, leisure, and wealth. The closer a person was to achieving these desires, the higher the person's status and perceived value.

Such a perspective leads to the pursuit of being number one in as many ways as possible and devalues other people, especially those who don't "measure up." So, to the Corinthians, the slaves, the poor, and the disabled were looked down upon. They were considered unworthy of honor, blessing, or care. Their lives were not valued; it didn't matter if they lived or died.

It is difficult to imagine a perspective more diametrically opposed to the worldview of God's kingdom. In God's kingdom the first shall be last; the leader is the servant of all; every person—no matter how weak, old, disfigured, poor, intellectually challenged, clumsy, or powerless—is made in the image of the Creator; and the King of kings and Lord of lords died a sacrificial death so that every person has the opportunity to experience an abundant life. So how does a follower of Jesus live as a citizen of heaven—God's kingdom—in a world where the values of Hellenism reign?

It was a difficult challenge for the Corinthians, and it is no less difficult for Jesus followers today. We too live in a Hellenistic culture and need to learn how to live out the values of God's kingdom in our world. In the following chart, consider the "culture" of Hellenism as it was lived in Corinth, and then describe how the "culture" of Hellenism is lived out in our world. Finally, thoughtfully and prayerfully describe what it looks like to be a living picture of the "culture" of God's kingdom as individual believers and as a community of God's people.

Values of Roman-Style Hellenism	Values of Our Culture's Hellenism (or, Humanism)	Cultural Values of God's Kingdom
Beauty or appearance: Sophocles wrote, "Wonders are many, and none is more wonderful than man."[10] The more beautiful a person was, the more he or she was worth.	Beauty or appearance:	Beauty or appearance:
Accumulation: the more you had, the more highly you were valued. Conspicuous consumption was the order of the day because public display of one's wealth gained status in the eyes of others.	Accumulation:	Accumulation:

(Cont.)

Values of Roman-Style Hellenism	Values of Our Culture's Hellenism (or, Humanism)	Cultural Values of God's Kingdom
Accomplishment: the more you accomplished and contributed to society, the more you were honored and respected. As Kostas Koliveras, the professor I studied with in Greece, said, "Corinth was a city where public boasting and self-promotion had become an art form."	Accomplishment:	Accomplishment:
A person's "following" or "entourage": for a price, wealthy patrons provided legal and protective services for "clients." The clients received food, clothing, money, etc., and in turn gathered around and followed the patron, providing public praise, support, status, and recognition.	A person's "following" or "entourage":	A person's "following" or "entourage":
Association with "lower" classes or the poor: Roman literature is filled with derogatory put-downs of slaves and the poor.[11] The poor had no honor or value and to associate with someone of a lower class or to work in a lower-class occupation was considered humiliating and demeaning.	Association with "lower" classes or the poor:	Association with "lower" classes or the poor:

Study 3 | The House Church Is the Body of Jesus

The Very Words of God

> *For just as each of us has one body with many members, and these*
> *members do not all have the same function, so in Christ we, though*
> *many, form one body, and each member belongs to all the others.*
>
> *Romans 12:4–5*

Bible Discovery

Live and Love Like the Body of Christ!

Love and unity always have been distinguishing marks of the community of God's people. God called Israel to live in unity and love their neighbors, and Jesus taught his disciples to love their neighbors and their enemies as well. Unity and love for one another authenticate the message Jesus commanded his followers to take to the entire world. Paul was absolutely convinced that the culture of the house church—the community of God's people in Corinth—must be characterized by love and unity if they were to present the kingdom of heaven as an alternative to Corinth's Hellenistic culture. As a trained rabbi, he looked for a metaphor to clearly convey his teaching on the unity God intended for the community of his people.

Where he found that metaphor might come as a bit of a surprise.

Corinth was home to a large temple complex dedicated to Asklepios, the Greek god believed to heal all human ills, relieve pain, and even raise the dead.[12] In the first century, people flocked to hundreds of such worship centers located throughout the Roman Empire. Asklepios centers were the hospitals of the day, combining religious ritual with a variety of herbal and water treatments, exercise, stress relief, prescribed diets, and drug-induced dream states for insight into healing.

In Corinth the Asklepion was located north of the agora. Functionally it could be described as a combination hospital, religious shrine, spa, and country club. The sanctuary complex comprised a temple with an altar for sacrifice, a sleeping chamber (*abaton*) where the healing dreams took place, treatment rooms, baths, a theater, a library, two rectangular rock pits apparently for the god's sacred snakes, and a colonnaded portico with multiple banquet rooms (*triclinia*) for eating the ritual meal following sacrifices offered at the temple.

In addition to these practices, visitors who sought healing would leave votive offerings in gratitude to the god or as a petition for his blessing. Made of clay or marble, these offerings depicted various human body parts and were placed around the temple perimeter. The one small area that has been excavated included nearly one thousand such offerings representing hands, feet, arms, legs, genitalia, heads, eyes, ears, and more! Anyone passing by would have seen an immense collection of disconnected body parts around the temple. It seems that Paul saw them too[13] and found them to be an apt metaphor for the lack of unity and truncated function that was occurring in the house church communities. Let's consider how Paul used this unusual metaphor to appeal for change in Corinth's house churches.

1. The dissension and division in Corinth's house church communities was the very opposite of the culture God wanted his people to demonstrate to a world in chaos. Paul needed to teach the importance of unity in the community of God's people—unity between each believer and recognition of each believer's unique gifts and role in the mission of making God known. This must have been a significant issue because Paul addresses it in the longest teaching homily of his letters to Corinth.[14]

   a. Even though God gives different gifts for different works of service, what is the unifying source and purpose of every gift the Spirit of God distributes to every believer? (See 1 Corinthians 12:1–11.)

In what ways was this different from the way the Corinthians typically viewed and used their abilities and talents? *Self/Chosen*

  b. No matter how many times Paul explained it, the Corinthians struggled to see themselves as a unified—but also diverse—community in which no one person was better, more honorable, or of a higher class than the others. Why do you think it was difficult for them to accept the unifying work of God's Spirit among them? (See 1 Corinthians 12:12–14.)

  c. Which absurd propositions did Paul pose to emphasize his points about how God intends the body of Christ to function? (See 1 Corinthians 12:15–26.)

What is Paul's message to believers who think they are not valuable in the body of Christ?

What is his message to believers who view their gifts as more important than the gifts of others?

Whose authority is being challenged when members of the body think they have a better idea of how the body should function and which gifts are the "best"?

2. The constant pressure to maintain class and one's status meant that compassion for the plight of others was not highly valued in the Corinthian culture. In fact, people of higher classes believed they deserved and had a right to the good life. They viewed the suffering of the lower classes as an issue the lower classes needed to address themselves. (See 1 Corinthians 12:25–26.)

   a. How hard do you think it would be for people in Corinth to learn to share in the suffering of others and to rejoice in the recognition of others?

  b. How hard is it for us to be imitators of Jesus who care deeply about our suffering brothers and sisters and are willing to "suffer with those who suffer"?

  c. When Jesus followers suffer with those who suffer, what do they communicate about God's love and character?

PROFILE OF A CULTURE
The Agape Love of the Body of Christ

Paul concluded his lesson on what it means to be the body of Jesus with what has become one of the most well-known passages in the Bible: 1 Corinthians 13.[15] We most frequently use this chapter at weddings as a model for marital love, but Paul originally intended to describe love as a pattern for all of life, particularly in relationships between believers. His lesson presents the antidote for dissension and division within the body of Christ.

First, Paul presents the problem: the Corinthians' lack of unity in the celebration of the Lord's Supper shows that they are living by the cultural norms of the pagan world. So Paul elaborates on the purpose and practice of the sacramental meal, and instructs them on how to repent and live in the love and unity Jesus expects. Then Paul discusses the nature of the one body and concludes with a powerful explanation of the importance of love between believers as a witness to the world of God's better way.

Ken Bailey's exceptional treatment of this passage notes the significance of Paul's word choice for love: *agape*. Normally the Greeks used two words for love: *eros* for passionate love and *phileo* for the love between close friends. By using *agape*, Paul gave an uncommon word new meaning. Bailey notes the qualities of *agape* love:

- *Agape* reaches out for everyone—spouse, friend, neighbor, and even our enemies.

- *Agape* is the great commandment for love of God and neighbor, the essence of the culture of the body of Christ.

- *Agape* is the love God demonstrated when he sent his Son, the love Jesus showed for his own, and the love Jesus' disciples are to imitate.

- *Agape* is the indispensable foundation of all of God's gifts to his people— greater than faith and hope.

- *Agape* is the gift of God's Spirit within us by which we are able to love others.

As you meditate on this chapter, notice that our gifts and acts of devotion are nothing if they are not rooted in *agape*. Be certain that *agape* is always selfless: patient, kind, without pride or self-promotion, truth seeking, and always seeking the best for others. *Agape* is primarily an action, not a feeling. *Agape* is greater than all other gifts because God is love. He loves us and empowers us to love one another. *Agape* never fails.

3. The self-serving Corinthian lifestyle created contention and division in what God intended to be a unified community of his witnesses. The new believers who joined God's community in Corinth still lived by the belief that people of higher status, greater wealth, exceptional beauty, or extraordinary accomplishment had greater worth. In fact, this is the first issue Paul addressed in his letter to the Corinthians.[16] Their lack of mutual love and respect for one another as individuals equally created in God's image posed a significant risk to the mission of making God known.

Their self-serving, cultural behaviors even crept into the celebration of the Lord's Supper. Instead of reminding the believers of Jesus' sacrifice that united them in the family of God, the holy meal of reconciliation Jesus instituted had become like a pagan banquet! Which specific behaviors that were common to Corinthian banquet practices led Paul to say that the house church gatherings were doing more harm than good? (See 1 Corinthians 11:17–19; 11:20–21.)

4. Paul made it clear that participating in the Lord's Supper as the Corinthians were doing was a grave offense against God. How did he describe it? (See 1 Corinthians 11:27.)

FOR GREATER UNDERSTANDING
Properly Discerning the Body

The importance of the body of Christ is a major theme in Paul's teaching letters to the Corinthian believers. He instructs them to remember that they meet together because of what Jesus did for them. Jesus broke bread and passed a cup of wine as symbols of their redemption, the new covenant God made with them through the sacrifice of Christ's body. Unfortunately, the Corinthians' lack of unity as a community of believers led to quarreling, division, and preferential treatment for some but disregard for others that resulted from their failure to recognize that the body of Christ extended not only to their relationships with one another but to their celebration of the Lord's Supper. Eating the communal meal without being "Christ's body" was displeasing to God and would compromise their witness to the pagan community.

It was not enough for the Corinthians to identify the meaning of the meal; they must live as a united body. The image of the "body"—Jesus' own crucified body and the church which is his body—is inseparable because our love for others is the result of Jesus' love for us and our faith in him. For this reason, self-examination and discernment (or proper recognition) of the body are essential. Eating and drinking the sacramental meal while also destroying the unity of the body through our attitudes or behavior may bring God's judgment. The celebration of the Lord's Supper was not to be another *convivum*—a class-conscious Roman banquet followed by a drinking party. Believers came together to remember the saving power of Jesus' body that made them his body—his church in the world. The "culture" of their celebration was inseparable from the "culture" of their living witness of God's better way.

5. To correct the pagan values being practiced during the Lord's Supper in the house churches, what did Paul carefully explain to them about what it mean to "discern the body"? (See 1 Corinthians 11:23–26.)

What specific things did Paul explain that the Corinthians must consider and do in order to "discern the body of Christ" and participate in the Lord's Supper properly? (See 1 Corinthians 11:28–34.[17])

6. In his prayer after the Last Supper with his disciples, Jesus prayed intensely regarding his mission and the mission his followers would carry forward after his death and resurrection. His prayer gives us a beautiful picture of Jesus' love and his unity with the Father. His prayer also shows that there is nothing more essential to the message spoken and lived than love, unity, and harmony within the community of God's people. Read John 17:1–23, and consider how Jesus' love for his followers provides a foundation that ought to encourage love and harmony in the hearts of his followers for one another.

    a. What did Jesus consider his mission to be? (See John 17:1–5.)

    b. In addition to praying for his disciples' protection, what experience that Jesus shared with his Father did Jesus want them to experience too? (See John 17:6–15.)

    c. Who else did Jesus pray for, what did he pray for them, and why? (See John 17:20–23.)

How does this prayer help you to understand Paul's passionate plea for unity and harmony in the house churches of Corinth?

What impact does it have on how you view and interact with the community of believers with whom you associate?

Reflection

Little is more devastating to the body of Christ than when its members do not, cannot, or will not get along. Division and discord in the body are cancers that undermine the well-being and mission of the very community God has chosen to be his partner in restoring *shalom* to hurting and broken people. Division and discord shatter the unity and harmony that ought to reign in the community of God's people—on earth as it is in heaven. If we live in disharmony, conflict, division, and dissension with one another, we end up proving that our message of God's love is not true! Instead of making God's love and character known in the world, we end up showing how broken we are and that the faith we proclaim is fraudulent.

There's no doubt that followers of Jesus today are concerned about the church and its witness in the world. We express concern about the disintegration of cultural values, the onslaught of immorality in entertainment, and a general public acceptance of ungodliness. We are concerned about our culture's impact on the church. I, too, am deeply concerned about the direction of our culture, but I think the discord—and at times hatred—that we harbor toward our brothers and sisters in the body of Christ is more destructive than outside cultural influences.

We need to allow Paul's metaphor for the community of Jesus followers in Corinth as the "body" of Jesus to speak to us. This timeless image is as meaningful for followers of Jesus today as it was in the first century. The body of Christ is designed to function as a whole—every part working together as its Creator intended—in order to fulfill its mission as God's partner in redeeming and restoring a world shattered by sin.

Without love, the body of Jesus cannot work as intended. God wants his people to recognize and respect the contribution of every member of Christ's community—our own as well as that of others. Imagine the potential if we, in fellowship together as the body of Jesus, lived out our faith with selfless cooperation, mutual respect, and loving appreciation for one another.

Psalm 133:1 exclaims, "How good and pleasant it is when God's people live together in unity!" This is what God desires for his people, his witnesses in the world, today. He pours out his blessing where such harmony exists. The question is, will we join together in love and be living witnesses of the harmony that comes when God's transforming power changes our hearts?

> To what extent do you live as if you are knit together with other believers in the way the Bible describes?

> What are we missing out on when we insist on exercising our gifts as autonomous individuals (or congregations) rather than as equal and necessary parts of the body of Christ in our communities?

What do you think would change if each member of the body of Christ believed that his or her gifts and the gifts of others were equally important and necessary for the church to function and fulfill its mission?

In what ways does this encourage you to more actively exercise your particular gift in your faith community?

In what ways might you be a better partner in the mission by:
- Using your gift with humility?

- Encouraging others to use their gift?

- Appreciating others for their labor for God's kingdom?

TRANSFORMING THE CHAOS

I have had the remarkable blessing and honor of teaching high school for more than forty years. The school in which I teach is committed to educational excellence and to challenging students to transform a broken world for Jesus. In that context, I have been greatly enriched by a significant number of dedicated students who are deeply committed disciples. But many of them anticipate their future path with some anxiety regarding how they will live out their commitment to share their faith in a broken world and to demonstrate what living for the Lord looks like every day.

I wonder if Paul had similar concerns as he anticipated making God known in Corinth. When Paul visited the city, it was a strategically located cosmopolitan center of nearly half a million people from every corner of the Roman Empire. It was notoriously immoral, known for its lavish wealth, wild parties, and sexual excess. If Paul could establish a community of Jesus followers in that environment, it would be possible to do so anywhere! A community of Jesus followers in Corinth would stand out like a city on a hill, a beacon of light displaying the transforming power of Jesus to the world. But was it possible? No wonder, especially after his disappointing experience in Athens, Paul came to Corinth with "fear and trembling."

But Paul soon discovered that God had prepared the way ahead of him. He met believers who shared his tent-making profession and provided a job and a house church community that met in their home. His faithful coworkers, Timothy and Silas, soon joined him in sharing the good news. Despite some difficult struggles, Paul's work was blessed beyond what he had seen in any of the cities he had visited previously. Many people believed the message, and in the most unlikely of places a community of Jesus followers grew and flourished.

Soon, however, the house church communities discovered what many of my students must learn as well. A deep commitment to share one's faith must be grounded in the lifestyle that faith demands. If the lives of believers are no different from those who do not share the faith, their witness to the world is destroyed. Many believers in Corinth, for instance, had not fully abandoned their pagan lifestyle. They misunderstood their freedom as believers and thought they had the "right" to do anything. Others continued participating in the sexual practices that had made their city famous. Such cultural conflict within the community of believers led to dissension, division, and a lack of unity that would destroy their witness if not corrected.

So Paul wrote to these special believers who lived in a very broken culture and needed to learn how to live out their faith. He taught them how to be holy people in their world. He taught them to give up certain sexual practices, to no longer participate in temple banquets, to care for those who suffered, and to love one another as equals. His writings give us a window into what their lives were like and how dramatic a lifestyle change they needed to make in order to honor their Messiah and become effective witnesses. It was not easy for them, just as it is not easy for my students and all believers, to be set apart as witnesses of God's kingdom while living in and engaging with a broken culture. Yet their struggles and their faithfulness are an example to help us do the same.

Opening Thoughts (3 minutes)

The Very Words of God

To the church of God in Corinth, to those sanctified in Christ Jesus and called to be his holy people, together with all those everywhere who call on the name of our Lord Jesus Christ—their Lord and ours.

1 Corinthians 1:2

Think About It

How challenging is it to learn a completely different way of doing something we have always done? For example, if a person has only driven a car with an automatic transmission, what happens when he or she gets behind the wheel of a car with a manual transmission? Or, what happens when a right-handed person injures that hand and has to relearn how to eat, get dressed, and write with the other hand?

It isn't easy. People who have learned one way of doing things may have no idea how to take different action.

What needs to happen in order for people to function successfully when everything they have learned and experienced undergoes a dramatic change?

Video Notes (31 minutes)

To be a Corinthian

Decadence

Sexual

Alcohol

To follow Jesus in the city of Aphrodite

Morality and faithfulness in marriage

Meat sacrificed to idols

Banquets

The Serapeion, temple to the Egyptian god Serapis

Meat sacrificed to idols and sold in the agora

versus

Meat sacrificed to idols and eaten in celebration of the god

Symposion—celebration of the god in the temple with gorging, drinking, and entertainment

Warnings about the immorality of temple feasts

Being the message—the synagogue on Delos

You live in Corinth, too

You are the sermon; be the alternative!

" Being " the message ·

Video Discussion (7 minutes)

1. We've learned a bit about the Hellenistic lifestyle as it was practiced in the Roman Empire, particularly in Athens and Corinth. How does your understanding of the situation Paul addressed in his letters to the Corinthians change when you realize that to be identified as a "Corinthian" was synonymous with drunkenness, sex workers, sexually transmitted diseases, and the most immoral behavior known in the Roman Empire?

2. On the map of Corinth note the Acrocorinth, a stone mountain that towers nearly two thousand feet above the ancient city. It is the dominant feature of the landscape, visible from every part of Corinth. The temple of Aphrodite, where the ancient writer Strabo claimed a thousand prostitutes served her worshipers, stood on top of the Acrocorinth as a highly visible symbol of Corinth's Hellenistic culture. How difficult do you think it would be to live out the mission as a follower of Jesus in the city of Aphrodite?

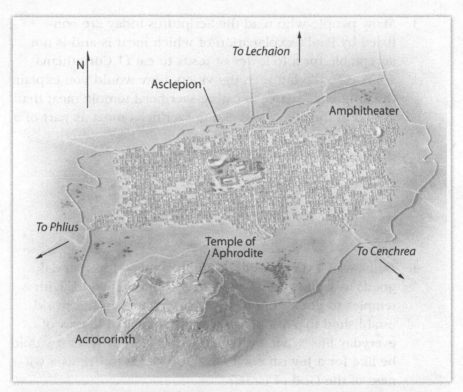

THE ACROCORINTH WHERE THE TEMPLE OF APHRODITE WAS LOCATED STANDS HIGH ABOVE THE CITY.

3. Many people who read the Scriptures today are con-
   fused by Paul's explanation of which meat is and is not
   acceptable for a follower of Jesus to eat (1 Corinthians
   10:25–32). Having seen the video, how would you explain
   the difference between eating sacrificial temple meat that
   is sold in the agora and eating sacrificial meat as part of a
   temple banquet?

4. Delos was a very wealthy trading center—for material
   goods as well as for slaves—in the ancient world. With
   temples to gods from nearly every culture in the world
   established there, idolatry was an unavoidable part of
   everyday life. What are your thoughts about what it would
   be like for a Jewish community on Delos to live as a witness of the God of Israel?

Small Group Bible Discovery and Discussion (15 minutes)

Living Out the Mission of God in the City of Aphrodite

Corinth, like Philippi, was a Roman colony where life was lived
just as it was in Rome. Colonies were established in order to
provide a place for certain citizens to live and to spread the
desire for Roman culture. Colonies lived by the laws, privileges,
and benefits of Rome. Residents often had running water, paved

streets, fountains, theaters, arenas, gymnasia, and other benefits that increased the appeal of being Roman.

Paul's mission in Corinth was to plant a colony of God's kingdom—the church of Jesus—within the colony of Rome. Corinthians who put their faith in Jesus as Messiah, Savior, and Lord would become a colony of heaven that displayed the "culture" of God's kingdom by living out its values in daily life. This commitment to holiness was essential to the mission of being God's witnesses in Corinth. God calls everyone he redeems to a life of godliness, not only out of gratitude and obedience but because we have been called to the mission of becoming God's holy people who bear witness of his character and the *shalom* of his kingdom.

The pagan culture of Corinth and the holiness of the believers' house church were radically different. The very presence of a culture that was not motivated by the self-serving Hellenism of Roman privilege or by the Aphrodite-inspired excesses of sexual pleasure was a critique of the Corinthian lifestyle and culture. A clash of cultures—mockery, belittling, and eventually persecution by those who lived as "citizens" of Rome in Corinth—was inevitable. But Paul's greatest concern for the community of Jesus followers in Corinth was not the opposition they might face. Rather, his greatest concern was that they would not fully leave behind the culture of Corinth and live as witnesses of God's better way. If they did not separate themselves from their previous lifestyle and learn to live as God's holy witnesses—a colony of heaven in Corinth—they could not fulfill the mission of making God and the *shalom* of his kingdom known in that city.

In our previous study, we explored how difficult it was for the Corinthian believers to set aside their cultural views of class and status and become unified as one in the body of Christ. Let's now consider the challenge believers who came to faith from a culture famous for its sexual excess faced as they discovered God's better way of sexual purity and godliness. Since sexual purity was a radically countercultural idea in Corinth, the city of Aphrodite, such a transformation could be accomplished only by a total commitment to faith and the transforming power of the Holy Spirit.

1. Hellenism is a worldview that assumes human reason is
    the ultimate source of truth and authority in the universe.
    The Greek philosopher Protagoras (481–411 BC) simply
    stated, "Man is the measure of all things of what is and
    what is not." With that foundation, the Greeks shaped the
    world with a culture devoted to the supremacy of human
    beings and human accomplishment. But as much credit as
    the Greeks might feel they deserve, Hellenism really didn't
    begin with them! What momentous choice did Satan present
    to Adam and Eve in the Garden of Eden? (See Genesis 3:1.)

    Satan posed this question after God had commanded,
    "But you must not eat from the tree of the knowledge of
    good and evil, for when you eat from it you will certainly
    die" (Genesis 2:17). So, what paradigm-changing choice
    did Adam and Eve make regarding who in the universe
    "is the measure of all things" and has the right to decide
    what is true, right, and best in the world?

    People who are raised in a Hellenistic (humanistic) culture
    find the temptation to do what is best in their own minds
    irresistible. Why do you think it is so difficult for us to
    acknowledge God as Lord of all (even our daily life choices)?

2. Given the culture of Corinth, where the human mind and
    its desires were the highest values and the worship of
    man-made idols was expressed through sexual indulgence,
    it would not be easy for new followers of Jesus to become
    the witnesses God called them to be. Their first order of
    business, of course, would be to recognize and choose
    God as their ultimate authority and source of wisdom for
    life. What is the Bible's fundamental teaching about God,
    his place in the universe, and the worship of idols? (See
    Exodus 20:3; Deuteronomy 6:13–17; 2 Kings 19:15; Psalm
    96:4–5; Isaiah 42:8.)

What possible justification is there for anyone who claims to
accept God as Creator and Lord of all to engage in idolatry?

PROFILE OF A CULTURE
Aphrodite, the Goddess of Love

Aphrodite, whose name is taken from *aphros*, or sea foam, is the Greek goddess
of love, beauty, seduction, and sexual pleasure. In the more acceptable myth of
her origin, Cronus castrated his father, Uranus the sky god, and threw his genitals
into the sea, creating the foam from which Aphrodite then emerged. Zeus was
afraid that the gods would fight over her, so he married her to the "deformed"
god, Hephaestus. Aphrodite, however, was unfaithful with many gods and mor-
tals, and the myths about her are very obscene (and remarkably modern).

Aphrodite represented lust, promiscuity, and love without relationship, bound-
ary, or consequence. She rejected all suitors in her search for pleasure, but

never found a permanent partner. As one might expect, worship practices of the Aphrodite cult were very sexual in nature. In addition to the sacrifices, ceremonies, and worship, ritual prostitution was practiced, which few people in the Roman Empire other than the Jews viewed as immoral. Sexual union with temple prostitutes represented a sacred marriage with the goddess that promised increased virility and fertility to the participant. At the height of her popularity, the historian Strabo claims more than a thousand male and female prostitutes were associated with her temple on the summit of the Acrocorinth.

There is little doubt that the worship of Aphrodite in Corinth contributed to an atmosphere of sexual excess and experimentation that became world famous. In addition to her temple on the Acrocorinth, there were at least two additional temples dedicated to her in the city. The worship of other gods such as Dionysus (the god of wine) and Hera (the goddess of the sexual life of women) also encouraged immorality. Thousands of "pilgrims" came to indulge in the sacred rituals celebrated in Corinth's temples. Its role as a wealthy port city with a "healthy" sex trade also fed Corinth's reputation for indulgence in unrestrained pleasure.

People from around the Roman Empire came to Corinth by the thousands to spend money and enjoy the multitude of socially acceptable pleasures. In addition to the temple prostitutes, *hetairai*, high-priced and skilled call girls, provided services that included cultural entertainment for temple banquets and private dinners. A host of ordinary prostitutes staffed brothels that lined the side streets and the forum. In addition, Corinthians consumed an enormous amount of wine.[1] So Paul worked very hard to counter the Corinthian attitude that "I have the right to do anything"[2] and teach the house church communities the importance of choosing to worship God over idols and choosing to obey his commands rather than their own desires.

3. The sin of idolatry is not only an affront to God, Creator and Lord of all, but it also destroys the mission and kingdom culture of his people because it leads to immorality, bloodshed, and a lack of concern for others.

a. Consider, for example what happened when the Hebrews created an idol in the form of a golden calf—not unlike the Egyptian cow goddess, Hathor—and sacrificed to it while Moses was on the mountain receiving God's revelation. How did they celebrate following the sacrifice? (See Exodus 32:6.)

b. What was the connection between idolatry and immorality in Numbers 25:1–3?

c. When Israel was enticed to serve the fertility gods of the Canaanites, Ba'al and Asherah, in which ungodly practices did they participate? (See Isaiah 57:5–6.)

d. What does the Word of the Lord given to Jeremiah reveal about what happens when his people, whom he has commanded to "love your neighbor as yourself" (Leviticus 19:18), choose instead to "follow other gods to your own harm?" (See Jeremiah 7:5–7.)

4. The biblical truth that there is one God and Creator who
    alone is worthy of our worship is not only a theological
    fact, it is a call to mission! When God created human-
    kind in his image (Hebrew, *tselem*), he created a physical
    representation of himself for the purpose of declaring
    his presence and revealing his nature or character. So, by
    virtue of our very nature—created in God's image—God
    built into us the mission to make him known and display
    his character. In Jewish thought, this principle undergirds
    the holiness in sexual practices that the Text emphasizes.
    As God's creation made in his image, we must care for
    ourselves (as God's *tselem*) in the way(s) God intended.
    This includes our physical care and sexual conduct.

    a. What impact ought the realization that immorality
        destroys our God-given mission to make him known
        in the world have on our motivation to pursue sexual
        purity and develop moral character?

    b. Considering the vast differences between the Hellenistic,
        idol-worshiping culture of Corinth and the culture of
        unity, *shalom*, kindness, and self-control characteristic
        of God's kingdom, what hope did the new believers in
        Corinth have that they could be faithful in their devotion
        to God? (See 2 Corinthians 3:18.)

Faith Lesson (3 minutes)

Encouraged by the social norms and religious values of a Hellenistic worldview, Corinth became famous for its hedonistic lifestyle. People valued pleasure and pursued the happiness of satisfying their desires as the ultimate goal in life. They believed everyone had the right to do whatever achieved the greatest pleasure, regardless of what it might cost other people.

The message of Jesus, however, is rooted in a different worldview. In keeping with Jesus' command to his disciples to teach others to "obey everything I have commanded you,"[3] his followers have a mission to establish an alternative culture that represents and displays God's nature and character to the world. That culture of godliness reveals how *shalom* flourishes when people stop living as they choose and commit to living as God intends.

So Paul went to Corinth, into the chaos of human vice, seeking to create a community that would reject the pagan ways of Hellenism in order to be a living example of moral restraint, sexual purity, sobriety, and compassion for others. And God's Spirit blessed his teaching, as many who had not found meaning in the temples or alleyways of Corinth believed and joined God's great story of redemption! By the faithfulness of other disciples and early followers of Jesus, this transformation from Hellenism to godliness took place in small communities of new believers throughout the Roman world. Community by community, city by city, God's kingdom was reclaimed from the Evil One.

Peter described the expansion of God's kingdom (1 Peter 4:2–3) this way:

> As a result, they do not live the rest of their earthly lives for evil human desires, but rather for the will of God. For you have spent enough time in the past doing what pagans choose to do—living in debauchery, lust, drunkenness, orgies, carousing and detestable idolatry.

Isn't this the transformation we long to see in our culture? Isn't this our mission as well?

1. Why is your life witness an effective "sermon" in a culture that often rejects God's authority?

   What will it take for you to be that "sermon"?

2. To what extent do you think followers of Jesus today present a viable, authentic alternative to the chaos of our culture?

   What must we learn, and which specific changes must we make in order to live the alternative culture Jesus redeemed us to represent?

Closing (1 minute)

Read 2 Corinthians 3:18 aloud together: "And we all, who with unveiled faces contemplate the Lord's glory, are being transformed into his image with ever-increasing glory, which comes from the Lord, who is the Spirit."

Then pray, thanking God that he created us in his image so that we might represent and display him to the world. Thank him for redeeming us and restoring us as his partners in bringing the *shalom* of his kingdom to those who are held captive to the culture of the Evil One's kingdom. Pray for faithfulness as we seek to leave behind the baggage of our former lives that destroys our witness. Pray for the power of God's Spirit to transform us into his image so that our lives will become the cultural alternative that leads people to know and glorify their Creator.

Memorize

> *And we all, who with unveiled faces contemplate the Lord's glory, are being transformed into his image with ever-increasing glory, which comes from the Lord, who is the Spirit.*
>
> **2 Corinthians 3:18**

Making God Known in a Broken World

In-depth Personal Study Sessions

Study 1 | Flee Immorality! Flee Idolatry!

The Very Words of God

> *Therefore, since we have these promises, dear friends, let us purify*
> *ourselves from everything that contaminates body and spirit, perfecting*
> *holiness out of reverence for God.*
>
> 2 Corinthians 7:1

Bible Discovery

Pursue the Mission! Live as God's Holy People

When Jesus gave his final lesson to his disciples before ascend-
ing to the Father, he instructed them to go to all nations and
teach them to obey everything he had taught them. And when
the Holy Spirit, as Jesus had promised, empowered them to carry
out the mission of making God known to the world, they went.
Likewise, when Jesus personally commissioned Paul to be a witness to the Gentiles, Paul pursued the mission, taking the gospel
message into the Gentile world.

Paul's obedience to Jesus' command eventually brought him to
Corinth where many Corinthians eagerly responded to the gospel. So Paul began teaching them, by word and by the example
of his life, to obey all that God had commanded and Jesus had
taught and demonstrated. He knew that as new disciples of Jesus,
the believers in Corinth were called to live as God's witnesses in
the pagan culture of their city. Just as God had called Israel out
of Egypt, set them apart to be his holy people, and given them
the mission of portraying his character and demonstrating his

love to the pagan nations around them, Jesus did the same for all who would become his disciples. Jesus commanded his followers to obey everything he taught so that they also would be a holy people set apart to be his witnesses and continue the mission of making God and his redemption known throughout the world.

From Paul's rabbinic training and extensive study of the Text, he knew that the holiness God desired from the believers in Corinth would not happen unless they abandoned their pagan gods. The Jewish sages taught that idolatry always led to immorality, and Paul certainly could cite many, many examples of that destructive progression recorded in the Hebrew Bible. Since the followers of Jesus who gathered in the house churches born through Paul's ministry in Corinth were called to be God's holy people—living models of his kingdom—their commitment to holy living was crucial to their mission. Living a holy life would be impossible if they worshiped idols and engaged in the immorality that accompanied it.

So Paul taught them to flee, or sprint away from, idolatry. That wasn't as easy as it might appear, however. Idol worship wasn't confined to one's personal religious practices, but permeated every aspect of Corinthian life—political, economic, and social. How would it be possible to live a holy life without withdrawing from society? How would it be possible to engage their pagan neighbors and avoid their immorality at the same time?

1. In order to better understand Paul's teaching to the Corinthian house churches regarding their call to holy living, we must go back in time to when Israel camped at the foot of the mountain in the Desert of Sinai. There, God's great story of redemption took a pivotal step forward when he called Israel to be his partners in restoring *shalom* to his sin-shattered creation. What specifically did God call Israel to be, and what was the condition of that calling? (See Exodus 19:2–6, especially 5–6.)

Why was this call to holiness necessary for the mission of representing God to the world? (See Leviticus 11:44–45; 19:2.)

What does the holiness of God's people prove to the world? (See Ezekiel 20:41.)

So, when Paul began his teaching letter to the Corinthian believers with the greeting, "To the church of God in Corinth, to those sanctified in Christ Jesus and called to be his holy people," what was he saying about them?

DID YOU KNOW?
To Be Kadosh

When God called his people to "Be holy because I, the Lᴏʀᴅ your God, am holy,"⁴ he commanded them to be *kadosh*, meaning holy in the sense of being distinct or set apart. He called them to leave behind the pagan cultural norms of Egypt and pursue a different way of life from what they had known. So that they would know how to do this, God followed his command with a long list of practices that would shape their lives and make them a distinct and holy people. God's instructions prohibited idolatry, required care for the poor and alien, taught how to treat others with love, and established standards for justice. In brief, these instructions taught Israel how to live in a way that imitated God's holiness. More than a millennium later, Jesus taught his disciples to be holy by imitating him.

---

2. God called Israel out of Egypt to be his holy people and gave them the entire book of Leviticus (as well as most of Numbers and Deuteronomy) to teach them how to live a holy life! In a similar way, Paul sent the Corinthian believers a letter of instructions on how to separate themselves from their sinful past so that they could learn to live as God's holy people. As a church community (*ecclesia*), they were set apart to be a holy people who pursued a life of very different values and behaviors from those they previously had known. But they found it difficult to separate themselves from the cultural practices of their former lifestyle. Paul did not underestimate the difficulty of their challenge. How did he (and Peter) describe the transformation that they and other believers from a pagan past were experiencing in order to be God's holy people? (See 2 Corinthians 6:14; Ephesians 5:8–12; 1 Peter 2:9.)

3. Corinth was famous for sponsoring the Isthmian Games, an Olympic-style athletic and music competition. Paul used an image of trained dedication and utmost effort applied toward a goal in order to emphasize to the Corinthian believers the urgency of pursuing holiness.

    a. From which behaviors did he urge them to run (*diokete*) away from, or flee? (See 1 Corinthians 6:18; 10:14.)

    b. How did he encourage them to run the race of obedience? (See 1 Corinthians 9:24, 26.)

4. Although the sexual practices of Corinth generally weren't considered immoral by Hellenistic or Roman standards, they were far out of bounds for the moral behavior God intended his human creation to enjoy.

    a. Why was the immoral behavior of the Corinthians destructive to the holy life God calls his people to pursue? (See 1 Corinthians 6:13, 18–20.)

    b. What place does immorality have in the kingdom of God, and to what lengths did Jesus go to purify his followers from it? (See 1 Corinthians 6:9–11.)

    c. The believers in Corinth needed to engage with people who didn't believe in order to demonstrate God's character and be a living testimony of life when it is lived according to the values of his kingdom. Even so, from what kind of engagement with unbelievers did they need to run? (See 1 Corinthians 6:14–18; 2 Corinthians 6:17.)

5. In addition to fleeing immorality, which other practice does Paul say to flee, and why was it a risk to a life of holiness? (See 1 Corinthians 10:1–7, 14; also Exodus 32:1–6.)

FOR GREATER UNDERSTANDING
Idolatry Leads to Immorality

In Paul's understanding, idolatry leads to a culture of immorality that affects all of life. Immoral rituals associated with idol worship, for example, also normalize immorality in daily life. If prostitution is part of our religious experience, sexual immorality must not only be permissible but desirable. Because idolatry was such a pervasive source of immorality in the Roman world, Paul taught that it must be avoided completely. His letters, as well as the writings of other biblical contributors, frequently warned of idolatry as a pathway to immorality.

You are to abstain from food sacrificed to idols, from blood, from the meat of strangled animals and from sexual immorality. You will do well to avoid these things.

ACTS 15:29

The wrath of God is being revealed from heaven against all the godlessness and wickedness of people, who suppress the truth by their wickedness. . . . For although they knew God, they neither glorified him as God nor gave thanks to him, but their thinking became futile and their foolish hearts were darkened. Although they claimed to be wise, they became fools and exchanged the glory of the immortal God for images made to look like a mortal human being and birds and animals and reptiles.

Therefore God gave them over in the sinful desires of their hearts to sexual impurity for the degrading of their bodies with one another. They exchanged the truth about God for a lie, and worshiped and served created things rather than the Creator—who is forever praised. Amen.

ROMANS 1:18–25

Put to death, therefore, whatever belongs to your earthly nature: sexual immorality, impurity, lust, evil desires and greed, which is idolatry.

COLOSSIANS 3:5

The acts of the flesh are obvious: sexual immorality, impurity and debauchery; idolatry and witchcraft; hatred, discord, jealousy, fits of rage, selfish ambition, dissensions, factions and envy; drunkenness, orgies, and the like. I warn you, as I did before, that those who live like this will not inherit the kingdom of God.

GALATIANS 5:19–21

6. The new Corinthian believers had lived under the assumption that they had the right to do anything they wanted and to live any way they wanted. In order to become God's holy people, however, they had to learn new priorities for living. What did Paul teach about their "rights" and what their first priorities should be? (See 1 Corinthians 8:9; 10:23–24.)

What needed to be the purpose and motivation for everything they chose to do? (See 1 Corinthians 10:31; also Matthew 5:16.)

Since the definition of a disciple is to follow the example of the rabbi in his walk with God, what did Paul invite the Corinthian believers to do in order to learn to live as holy people? (See 1 Corinthians 11:1; 1 John 2:6.)

7. Turning away from immorality and idolatry was not easy, and some of the Corinthian believers refused to change their ways. What impact would this conflict of values and lifestyle have on the testimony of the community of believers, and what did Paul insist they do about it? (See 1 Corinthians 5:9–11.)

Reflection

Like other itinerant Jewish rabbis of his time, Jesus taught through both his words and his actions, inviting his hearers to believe and follow him. Those who accepted his message as God's truth and chose to follow him then dedicated themselves to imitating the way he lived, or as it is also expressed, walking as Jesus walked.[5] Paul, who also was a Jewish rabbi, needed to teach the new Corinthian believers how to engage with people immersed in Corinth's pagan culture of idolatry and immorality and still live a pure and holy life that would be a living testimony of God's *shalom*. So Paul invited them to imitate him in order to know how Jesus lived. "Follow my example," he wrote, "as I follow the example of Christ."[6]

If we, as followers of Jesus in our world, are committed to living a holy life that is the kind of living witness we are called to be, we too need to imitate the example of Jesus. His mission was to put the *shalom* of God's kingdom on display, fulfill the sacrifice required for God's plan of redemption, and teach his disciples to carry on the mission of making God known in a broken world. So Jesus spent most of his time teaching the Jewish people in Galilee. However, his reputation for wisdom, love, and godliness was so widespread that even Gentiles sought him out. And on occasion he left Galilee and engaged with the Gentile world, teaching and healing wherever he went.

Even though Jesus was severely criticized by the religious establishment for interacting with sinners and Gentiles who were "unclean," he brought God's *shalom* to their world. He healed a Roman centurion's servant.[7] He exorcised a demon from the child of a pagan Canaanite woman.[8] He healed a deaf man in the Decapolis.[9] And for the Roman centurion who watched him die on the cross, Jesus' living testimony—even in an agonizing death—convinced him that Jesus was the Son of God![10] Are we willing to follow Jesus' example and be set apart as holy people and living witnesses of God's character and *shalom* in our world?

Will you follow the example of Jesus and seek to live as he lived and imitate his love for people who do not know God?

How intentional are you about pursuing purity and holiness so that your life will be such a powerful witness of God's love and peace that people who live in our broken world will draw near to discover who God is?

Which parts of your life before you were washed clean and sanctified by Jesus do you need to run away from as fast as you can in order to become the living witness God has called you to be?

When we seek to live a holy life, we sometimes isolate from the very people God has called us to reach out to in his love. What do you learn about what it looks like to reach out to people who do not know God from the examples of Jesus reaching out to the Gentile world?

- How might you engage with your world through conversations or teaching?

- How might you engage with those who are sick, needy, or lonely?

- How might you engage with people who seem pleased to live an immoral life?

- How might you engage by bringing peace or hope to people who face difficult challenges?

Study 2 | Idolatry and Sacrificial Meat

The Very Words of God

> So whether you eat or drink or whatever you do, do it all for the glory
> of God. Do not cause anyone to stumble, whether Jews, Greeks or the
> church of God.

1 Corinthians 10:31–32

Bible Discovery

Do Not Cause Anyone to Stumble

After his time in Corinth, Paul spent several years teaching in
Ephesus, where it is believed he wrote his letters to the Corinthians. The Corinthian believers apparently had written to Paul
asking questions about their new life as followers of Jesus. His
letters are a collection of instructions on godly living personal-
ized for the challenge of being living witnesses of God and his
kingdom in the cultural setting of Corinth. So it is not surprising
that Paul provided an extensive lesson on sexuality, immorality,
and marriage as God intended.

What is unexpected is Paul's abrupt change of subject to explain
appropriate behavior related to eating meat that has been sacrificed to idols. Today's readers of Paul's letter likely wonder what
sexual morality has to do with what's on the menu! Although
we don't readily see the connection, the association made perfect sense to Jesus followers who lived in first-century Corinth.
Paul was not introducing a new subject; he was continuing
his instruction about maintaining sexual purity while living in
Corinth's flagrantly immoral culture.

Most people in Corinth at the time rarely ate meat, and when
they did, it inevitably was sacrificial meat linked to the worship
of idols. Some portions of sacrificial meat were removed from
the temple and taken to the agora to be sold to the public. Other
portions of the idol meat were eaten as part of the worship ritual
for the respective god, during which excessive consumption of

wine, followed by immoral entertainment, often occurred. To further complicate matters, such activities weren't limited to the dedicated worshipers of the gods.

Every vocational guild had a patron god or goddess, and all members were expected to be involved in celebrations honoring that god. Banquets sponsored by the higher classes to show off their wealth often were held in temple banquet halls and followed the established worship ritual and banquet format. Political status and power were often displayed and maintained by participation in such banquets as well. So participation in banquets where meat sacrificed to idols was eaten and where sexual immorality was the prescribed entertainment was a frequent event for residents of Corinth. Let's see how Paul instructed his beloved believers to deal with this threat to godly living and the testimony of the community of Jesus in Corinth.

1. As true Hellenists, the Corinthians were used to doing things their own way. The universe worked the way they decided it worked. They made life choices that suited themselves. And their rules were for their own benefit and self-preservation. Often the Corinthian believers struggled to step out of their decadent, self-serving mindset and lifestyle and learn to walk the path of obedience, moral purity, and love—to "walk as Jesus walked." Which underlying Corinthian cultural belief that created confusion and struggle when it came to pursuing a godly life of sexual purity did Paul address in 1 Corinthians 6:12–13?

FOR GREATER UNDERSTANDING
The Temple of Serapis

Serapis, a fusion of several Egyptian and Greek deities, was invented to be a unifying influence between Greeks and Egyptians. So it is not surprising that a temple complex to Serapis (Serapeion) was built on Delos, a key island port in the Aegean Sea linking Egypt to the Greek world. The Serapeion comprised a small temple structure (only six by eight feet) built over a spring, a courtyard, and other buildings surrounded by a low wall.

Three small altars and a moneybox for donations have been located in the courtyard in front of the temple. Beyond the altars was another building, the banquet or dining hall. Every temple complex had such a facility. What took place in the banquet hall was the focus of Paul's instructions regarding when and where followers of Jesus were permitted to eat sacrificial meat.

In the Serapeion, the banquet hall was sixteen by thirty feet. Marble benches lined its walls, providing space for about thirty diners to recline and enjoy their meal. An inscription on the front of the benches reminded participants that the benches were provided for the banquet to which Serapis had invited them. Worshipers and members of guilds that had chosen Serapis as their patron god would gather to offer the animal sacrifice. Then they would recline to eat the sacrificial meat and celebrate the drinking and entertainment (*symposion*) that followed.

2. Paul began his instructions regarding the consumption
    of meat sacrificed to idols by taking a shot at the Corin-
    thians' Hellenistic, know-it-all approach. In Greek, the
    grammatical structure he chose for 1 Corinthians 8:1–2
    indicates that he was addressing their opinion about what
    they thought they knew. (See 1 Corinthians 8:1–6.)

    a. What did Paul acknowledge the Corinthian believers
        knew about idols, and therefore, eating meat sacri-
        ficed to idols?

    b. What did Paul point to as the problem or weakness
        with their knowledge? (See verse 2.)

3. Which key limitation of the Corinthian believers' knowl-
    edge about eating meat sacrificed to idols did Paul point
    out as being potentially harmful to their brothers and
    sisters in the faith? (See 1 Corinthians 8:7–13.)

    How serious a problem did Paul consider this to be?

What personal example did Paul share with them in an effort to show them how to live a godly life for the benefit of the body of Christ and the advancement of their mission?

DID YOU KNOW?
Iobacchoi Column

This stone column found in Athens records the banquet regulations for an association devoted to the god, Dionysus. Like all banquets of the time, the *deipnon* of the Iobacchoi were designed to recognize each member's class and honor them accordingly. The column specifies exactly how to carry out the sacrifices to the god, that members are to be seated according to social rank, that sacrificial meat is distributed by class from the equestrian to the freed slaves, and that the order of service is by social status.

4. Paul's warnings and instructions regarding eating meat that has been sacrificed to idols are often confusing to contemporary readers. This is due in part to our English translations making no distinction between the early Christian use of the Greek words, *eidolothuton*, which refers to sacrificed meat that was eaten in the presence of the god (as part of the worship ritual and banquet that followed), and *hierothuton*, which simply refers to meat that has been sacrificed. With that distinction in mind, reread 1 Corinthians 10:18–28 and consider which type of meat Paul was referring to in his specific instructions.

   a. On what basis did Paul indicate sacrificial meat sold in the marketplace was permissible to eat? (See 1 Corinthians 10:19, 25–26; also Psalm 24:1.)

   b. Acknowledging that idols are not real gods, why did Paul strongly prohibit eating meat as part of the worship ritual for a god? (See 1 Corinthians 10:19–22.)

   c. Drawing on his knowledge of the Hebrew Text, why was Paul concerned about any association the Corinthian believers might have with demons that would arise from their participation in idol worship, which would include eating meat in the ritual banquet setting? (See Exodus 32:5–8; Leviticus 17:3–7; Numbers 25:1–3; Psalm 106:28.)

d. Paul's concern was not limited to the demon-inspired indulgence in immorality of individual believers who participated in idol worship rituals. What concern did he express for other members of the body of Christ, and what example did he give of how that concern influenced his own behavior? (See 1 Corinthians 10:27–33.)

PROFILE OF A CULTURE
Idolatry and Meat Sacrificed to Idols

People in the Roman Empire during the first century took their pagan religious practices very seriously. Success in life depended on achieving harmony with the gods, the invisible powers that while not all-powerful could prevent or cause disaster in one's daily life. So people went to great lengths to avoid offending their deities and to influence the gods to behave in a beneficial manner toward them. Unlike Jews and Jesus followers, worshipers of pagan deities had no concept of sin or moral failure in their religious practice. Their focus was on success, not sin. Morality was defined by cultural practice, not the requirements of the gods.

Nevertheless, pagan worshipers were highly motivated to avoid offending their deities, and appropriate performance of religious ritual—including sacrifices and the celebration that followed—was essential to that end. As a result, worship of pagan gods involved carefully scripted and elaborate ritual practices. Generally, the ritual began with a procession of worshipers, musicians, and priests leading the sacrificial animal to the temple. Then prayers, followed by washing, inspection, slaughter, offering, and distribution of the animal took place. This was all carefully done according to prescribed ritual. A mispronunciation, an inappropriate hand gesture, or any imperfection of the animal sacrifice could offend the deity and upset the harmony that was essential for a happy life.

Following the sacrifice and offering of meat on the god's altar, the remaining meat was either consumed in the temple banquet hall as a continuation of the ritual or was sold to the public. Paul's concern about meat sacrificed to idols focused on the meat eaten in the temple banquet setting as part of the worship ritual. These temple banquets—whether sponsored by the temple priests, a guild or other organization, or an individual—were elaborate feasts known as *symposia*, from the Greek root that meant "to drink together." While not every temple banquet involved excessive immorality, the practice was well known in Corinth where immorality was a way of life.

The Greek *symposion* began as parties where a small group of friends gathered for conversation while eating and drinking to excess, but by the first century the practice grew into the temple banquet format. First, an extravagant menu featuring the meat from the sacrificed animal was served. This part of the celebration, the *deipnon*, often included the wives and children of the celebrants. Following the meal, the women and children would leave and the serious drinking and entertainment began.

Entertainment could include poetry recitation, musical performance, dancing, and jugglers. In addition, female *hetaerae*, the equivalent of an escort service, provided companionship, intellectual conversation, and sexual pleasures. All the while, young boys served wine and provided sexual pleasure as well. Fueled by excessive drinking, one can only imagine the sexual activity—heterosexual and homosexual—that ensued.

Eating sacrificial meat in the temple banquet halls exposed participants to the full range of immorality that occurred. These were not isolated incidences. Guild feasts were held in the patron god's banquet hall on a regular basis. They were a normal part of business and social life for many. It was a great challenge for Jesus followers—called to be a holy people set apart to live godly lives as witnesses of God's kingdom to the pagan community—to engage with their culture without being drawn into the demon-influenced ungodliness practiced in the temple banquets.

5. We focused our study regarding the believer's consumption of sacrificial meat on the Corinthian experience. But this challenging problem in engaging culture while maintaining a holy witness to the community was not limited to Corinth.

   a. What dire warnings did John record in Revelation to the churches in Pergamum and Thyatira because of their tolerance of eating food sacrificed to idols? (See Revelation 2:14–16, 20–23.)

   b. What encouraging words did Paul write to the Thessalonian believers regarding how they turned away from their idolatrous past? (See 1 Thessalonians 1:7–9.)

Reflection

We live in an increasingly decadent culture—one that demands its own rights and serves its own desires above all else. While I am not familiar with any idol worshiping cults in my community, the principles Paul teaches about living as a community of God's holy people in a Hellenistic and idolatrous culture apply to us as well. We, too, need to learn to "walk as Jesus walked." We, too, need to turn away from the idols of our own making and be the faithful, holy bride of Christ. We, too, need to give up our own rights to bless our fellow believers.

The people of Paul's day wanted the same things we do: prosperity and happiness. They pursued those things by creating
and serving their idols. If God is not truly Lord of our lives, we
replace him with idols too. We may not serve statues or images,
but we serve idols like jobs, relationships, hobbies or sports,
"stuff," popularity or fame, and so much more.

> What are the idols you serve—the things that make you feel
> successful, happy, and good about life—that keep you from
> being fully devoted to the one, true God?

Believers who truly love one another refrain from any action
that might cause another believer to sin or abandon the faith.
That's why Paul was willing to be a vegan if it prevented another
believer from sinning. Promoting a sacrificial lifestyle that set
aside one's own needs for the sake of others must have been a
hard sell for Paul, because giving up anything for someone else
didn't come naturally to a Corinthian. And I think it may be a
harder sell for Western believers in the twenty-first century!

We are God's holy temple, one body, that functions well only if
all of its parts are well. If our members are weak in some aspect
of their walk with God, it isn't just "their" problem. It is a problem for the entire community of believers.

> What is your commitment to love other members of the body
> of Christ?

What sacrifices are you willing to make in order to bless your fellow believers, especially those who are struggling—and sometimes failing—to grow in their faith?

Study 3 | A Synagogue on Delos

The Very Words of God

"This is what I told you while I was still with you: Everything must be fulfilled that is written about me in the Law of Moses, the Prophets and the Psalms." Then he opened their minds so they could understand the Scriptures. He told them, "This is what is written: The Messiah will suffer and rise from the dead on the third day, and repentance for the forgiveness of sins will be preached in his name to all nations, beginning at Jerusalem. . . . But you will receive power when the Holy Spirit comes on you; and you will be my witnesses in Jerusalem, and in all Judea and Samaria, and to the ends of the earth."

Luke 24:44–47; Acts 1:8

Bible Discovery

Committed to Fulfilling the Mission

As Jesus had commanded him to do, Paul faithfully proclaimed the good news to the Gentile world. Many pagans in the city of Corinth responded to his message and came to know and experience Jesus as their Savior and Lord. The new believers who had worshiped pagan deities renounced their gods, gathered with other followers of Jesus in small house church communities, and, transformed by the power of God's Spirit, learned to live by the values and priorities of God's kingdom. Long held in bondage to the self-serving morality of the Evil One's kingdom, they found a new life of *shalom* in God's kingdom.

With grateful hearts, these new believers joined God's great redemption story and found a life of purpose and meaning they never imagined. They had a new role as God's holy people, called and commissioned to be a light in the darkness that was Corinth. Just like Paul, other Jesus followers, and a long history of faithful people God had chosen to be his witnesses, they were called to engage their culture and live like a "colony of heaven" in their city. They became God's living witnesses who, by their words and actions, revealed his character and showed what life looks like when his kingdom reigns. They were to the nonbelievers of Corinth what God had called Israel to be to the pagan nations around them.

Their assignment was not easy. Every life activity in Corinth— one's occupation, local politics, the marketplace, social gatherings, and every festival—was devoted to one pagan deity or another. How could they live as God's holy people and still participate in the daily life of their city? Was it even possible to imitate Jesus while living in the culture of Corinth? How could they live in that place and not compromise their God-given mission of making him known?

From the beginning of his great redemption story, God has redeemed his people by grace, given them a mission, empowered them by his Spirit, instructed them by his revelation, and encouraged them through the community of his people. As followers of Jesus we, like the believers of Corinth, may struggle to live as God's holy people in the communities in which God has placed us. But we can find great encouragement for pursuing our mission in the story of God's people who have pursued it before us. One reminder of their faithfulness is found in the ruins of an ancient synagogue in Delos.

The synagogue of Delos was a little "colony of heaven" in a wealthy, temple-ridden seaport. It stands as a testimony to the mission of making God known in places where the kingdom of the Evil One appears to reign with great power. It reminds us of the power of a godly life lived not for one's own gain, not for any pride in moral purity, but for the sacred purpose of advancing God's kingdom in a world reeling in chaos.

THE MOSES SEAT AND STONE BENCHES (CHIEF SEATS) IMMEDIATELY IDENTIFY THIS ANCIENT BUILDING ON DELOS AS A JEWISH SYNAGOGUE. DISCOVERED MORE THAN A CENTURY AGO, THIS IS ONE OF THE OLDEST SYNAGOGUES EVER FOUND, DATING TO 100 BC. IT REMAINS TODAY AS AN ARCHAEOLOGICAL EXAMPLE OF THE JEWISH COMMUNITY'S COMMITMENT TO LIVE A HOLY LIFE IN A PAGAN CULTURE.

1. God's plan of redemption is to bring all people to himself, redeem them by his grace, and restore them to live life as he intended it to be before sin turned his perfect creation into chaos. God chooses human partners to join him in the mission of making him known to those who have not experienced him. At Mount Sinai, he chose the Hebrew people, Israel, to be his holy people and kingdom of priests who by their every word and action would display his character to the world. What had God done for them, and what commitment did they make to him? (See Exodus 19:2–8.)

What has God done for everyone who follows Jesus, and what does he call followers of Jesus to be? (See 1 Peter 2:9–12.)

2. In the understanding of the ancient world, a "kingdom" is not necessarily a geographical location. It is any place where a king's will is obeyed. So a kingdom demonstrates what life looks like when the king reigns. What, then, had God called his people to do, and what kind of life was he asking them to live? (See Exodus 19:5–6.)

If God's people were faithful to their calling, what would people who did not know God see by witnessing how they lived?

Jesus said he was sent to "proclaim the good news of the kingdom of God" (Luke 4:43). What did he instruct his disciples to pray for, and what would happen if they were living models of the holiness and *shalom* of God's kingdom? (See Matthew 6:9–10; 13:31–33.)

If we, as Jesus followers today, are faithful to our calling to be living examples of God's kingdom on earth, what can we expect people who do not know God to see through our lives?

3. Ancient people understood names to be an expression of the essence of a person's identity, a description of their reputation and character. So when King David reaffirms God's calling on his people and says, "Give praise to the LORD, proclaim his name," what would be involved in doing that? (See 1 Chronicles 16:8.)

   Jesus taught those who would be his followers to speak and live in such a way that God would be honored and praised by others. As followers of Jesus, what is the worthy outcome we hope for in our relationships and interactions with others? (See Philippians 2:10–11.)

4. God's human partners are created in his image, so our very lives are intended to reflect God's nature and presence. But sin separated God's people from his holiness, so what did God command Israel to create so that he

could live among them and allow people to experience
the reality of his presence? (See Exodus 25:8.)

In what unique way has God transformed and con-
structed the community of Jesus followers to be his presence to those who do not know him? (See Acts 2:1–12;
1 Corinthians 3:16–17; Ephesians 2:19–22.)

5. What great privilege has God given to his chosen part-
    ners in redemption that provides purpose and meaning to
    everything they do in life? (See Isaiah 43:10–12.)

How did Jesus pass on this same privilege and mission to
his followers? (See Matthew 10:18; Acts 1:8.)

6. The chaos of life in the world because of sin is described in Scripture as living in darkness, and it is a grim picture. Isaiah 9:2 describes "people walking in darkness . . . those living in the land of deep darkness." In contrast, what does God say his holy people, his redeemed partners, are for those who live in that darkness? (See Isaiah 42:6.)

   What is essential for God's people to fulfill that role, and what has God committed to do to make that happen?

   In John 8:12, Jesus asserted his identity as the light of the world. What did Jesus also say about the identity of his followers, and what does that require of those of us who follow him? (See Matthew 5:14–16; Acts 13:47; Ephesians 5:8–11.)

7. Through this study we've reviewed the mission of God's people—the mission for Israel, the mission for the believers of Corinth, the mission for those of us who follow Jesus today.

a. Sometimes through several millennia of that history, we, as the community of God's faithful people, have been successful. We have lived in such a way that others have recognized the one true God. What powerful testimony to that faithfulness did Naaman, a pagan Syrian commander, proclaim after his encounter with God's prophet, Elisha? (See 2 Kings 5:15.)

b. At other times we have failed to live as God commands and have not been the witnesses our world desperately needs us to be. When Israel failed to be faithful to God and the mission to which he called them, he exiled them from the land he had given to them. They then found themselves as a tiny minority in very pagan places. Would they join the culture and lose their identity as God's people? Would they isolate and fail to carry out the mission? Would they engage with those foreign cultures and remain faithful to God and the mission? What hope and guidance do the prophet Jeremiah's instructions to Israel at that crucial crossroads provide to followers of Jesus today who find themselves as a small, seemingly insignificant community of witnesses in a culture of overwhelming chaos? (See Jeremiah 29:5–7.)

PROFILE OF A CULTURE
A Synagogue in an Unlikely Place

In about 1000–900 BC, the Ionians colonized the small island of Delos as a religious center. Although the island had no natural resources or means of producing food, it had natural harbors sheltered by nearby islands and, by 100 BC, had become a prime trading and financial center. Commercial activity on Delos at one point included the largest slave market in the Roman Empire, able to "admit and send away ten thousand slaves on the same day."[11]

At its peak, nearly thirty thousand people from around the Mediterranean, most of whom were wealthy merchant families and their slaves, lived on Delos. Residents built extravagant villas on the hillsides and enjoyed such Roman amenities as a stadium, gymnasium, and theater. In addition, they built temples to a number of deities, the most impressive of which was the sanctuary of Apollo. It featured three temples dedicated to Apollo, a sacred lake, a sanctuary to Dionysus, and many other smaller temples, altars, and monuments. Because of the island's legendary identity as the birthplace of the twin gods Apollo and Artemis, many pilgrims came to worship those deities in the sanctuary on Delos.

But in a residential center on the east side of the island, away from the commercial center and pagan temples was another sanctuary—a sanctuary that to this day is a testimony to the Jewish community that lived on Delos! This synagogue, built so close to the Aegean Sea that waves have washed some of it away, is believed to have been built in about 100 BC, making it one of the oldest synagogues ever found. As is true of most synagogues built while the temple in Jerusalem was still standing, the synagogue faces east. The larger of its two rooms is about fifty-five by fifty feet with marble benches lining the walls—likely the "chief seats" where the wisest in the community sat during Sabbath prayer. Still prominent in the ruins of the structure is an elaborately carved marble chair, believed to be the "Moses Seat" where the person reading the Torah would sit. The smaller room is likely the synagogue school. Stone water basins by the building are believed to be *mikveh*, used for ritual washing.

It is amazing to realize that God's people were on Delos too. They were yet another "colony of heaven" seeking to represent God and his kingdom in the midst of the commercial, religious, and social chaos of Roman Hellenism. Archaeologists have found inscriptions of thanks, vows, dedications, and donations to *Theos Hypsistos*, literally the "most high God," a term used to identify the God of the Jews. Apparently, God's faithful people on Delos made a significant enough impact to be recognized. Josephus writes that the Jews on Delos were exempted from military service.[12] In addition, the Jewish congregation on Delos is mentioned in the Apocrypha[13] as one of the locations to which Rome addressed letters declaring protection from anti-Semitism.

How did the Jewish community live in that culture and maintain their witness? First, they were people of the Text. The Torah went everywhere they went. It shaped and molded their lives much as the Roman Empire and a Hellenistic culture shaped the lives of the Gentiles. Their passionate devotion to Scripture and their commitment to obey God's commands kept them faithful to their mission. And we must not forget that they were a community. When God calls his people to live exemplary, righteous lives under difficult circumstances, it is only possible when they unite as a community to correct, model, and encourage one another.

Reflection

When I began this study series more than twenty-five years ago, I had no idea of the exhilarating journey God had prepared for me. I have been privileged, challenged, and blessed beyond anything I could have imagined. Even the name for this series, "That the World May Know," has exceeded my expectations. When asked to decide on a name for the study series, I knew only that I wanted the name to honor God and capture the essence of the message I hoped to pass on to others. So I thought, prayed, and talked with others.

Finally, while in Israel, I asked a Jewish friend and scholar who had mentored me what he thought. Without a moment's hesitation he said, "That the World May Know!" I asked why he chose that name, and he pointed to a distant hill where the Israelites had camped when David met Goliath in the valley below. My friend explained that as David prepared his sling to confront the giant, he told the giant how he was going to kill him and why: "That the whole world will know that there is a God in Israel!"[14] Then my friend added that David's motivation is the same motivation for all of God's people to live obedient lives.

My friend was right. God saves his people by grace and calls them to the mission of living as a picture of who he is and demonstrating through their life example what the *shalom* of God's salvation looks like. God commissions his people to cultivate *shalom* as an advertisement, a preview if you will, of the kingdom of heaven. And the Text is full of examples of God's faithful people who lived the mission in such a way "that the world may know." They lived in obedience to God's commands so that people who did not know God could experience an intimate knowledge of his presence that could change their lives forever. Consider their testimony:

- Why did Moses pray and stop the hail in Egypt even though he knew Pharaoh still would not fear God (Exodus 9:29–30)?

- How did Joshua explain the reason for the miracles God performed in bringing Israel safely to the Promised Land (Joshua 4:21–24)?

- In his praise to God at the dedication of the temple, why did Solomon pray for God to uphold Israel so that they would be faithful to their calling (1 Kings 8:56–60)?

- When Hezekiah and the remaining Israelites faced certain annihilation by the Assyrians, on what basis did he beg for God to deliver them (2 Kings 19:17–19)?

- In his final prayer for his disciples before he was crucified, what did Jesus promise to continue doing (John 17:25–26)?

These servants of God caught the mission. As God's holy people they lived as his witnesses. By their words and by their deeds they demonstrated his presence so that people living in the chaos of sin and darkness would experience (know) God through them. Now it is our turn.

I pray that you have personally known and experienced God's story of redemption and that you will take your place in this greatest of all stories. If you have been saved by grace, will you live as God commands so that you can be a channel of the restoring power of God's *shalom* to those who are living in the chaos and darkness of your world?

> What would it look like to live as a "colony of heaven" in the midst of the chaos of your immediate family, your neighborhood, your school, your workplace?

> What will you do to cultivate a picture of God's *shalom* in these places?

The world needs to hear your voice; it needs to see your example. It needs all of God's witnesses to engage with our broken world. It needs the presence of God in his people shining as a light in the darkness in the most challenging situations that exist on earth.

How deep is your commitment to learn how to live out the mission so that the world may know God and the *shalom* of his redeeming love?

What is the greatest weakness or obstacle in the testimony of your life example?

What next step will you take toward living out the mission with all your heart, mind, and strength so that the world may know God?

NOTES

Introduction

1. 1 Corinthians 12.
2. Sandra L. Richter, *The Epic of Eden* (Downers Grove, Ill.: Inter-Varsity Press, 2008), chapter 1; Kenneth E. Bailey, *Jacob and the Prodigal* (Downers Grove, Ill.: InterVarsity Press, 2003), chapter 1, sections 1 and 3. These each provide an excellent description of the need to understand and the proper use of the cultural setting of the Bible.
3. Acts 6:5; 13:43; Romans 16:5; 1 Corinthians 16:15.
4. Acts 15:36–16:4, 10. Paul chose Silas (the shortened version of Sylvanus) and Timothy to join him. In Acts 16:10, Luke the author switches from "they" to "we" in describing Paul's work, an indication that Luke joined them before they reached Philippi.
5. Philippians 1:2: "Grace and peace to you from God our Father and the Lord Jesus Christ."
6. Christopher J. H. Wright, *The Mission of God: Unlocking the Bible's Grand Narrative* (Downers Grove, Ill.: IVP Academic, 2006). For an excellent treatment of Jesus and the mission of Israel, see chapter 15, "God and the Nations in New Testament Vision."
7. John 17:6.
8. 1 Corinthians 11:1.
9. Matthew 5:14–16; 1 Peter 2:9–12.
10. 1 Corinthians 3:9.
11. Jeremiah 29:4–7.
12. Jonathan Sacks in a speech entitled "The Western World and

the JudeoChristian Revelation of God" presents a powerful vision of God working through his people who have little power or influence on their own. I find this idea compelling, given how tempting it is to seek to bring God's will by economic or political power rather than by faithful living.

13. Acts 23:6.

14. Acts 22:3.

15. Philippians 3:5; Acts 23:6.

16. Philippians 1:14.

17. Philippians 1:27.

Timeline

1. Not all scholars agree on some dates in the life of Paul. One of the most helpful timelines is found in Ben Witherington, *The Acts of the Apostles: A Socio-Rhetorical Commentary* (Grand Rapids: Eerdmans, 1998), 81–86.

2. According to the writings of St. Jerome, the great Church Father (342–420 AD), Saul's parents were originally from Gischala in northern Galilee. They apparently joined in a revolt against Rome and were exiled to Tarsus as slaves. Although this tradition is unsupported, Jerome is considered a reliable source. The Romans exiled Jewish slaves from northern Galilee in 61, 55, 52, and 4 BC and 6 AD. Saul's parents then would have been freed from slavery— made "freedmen"—in order for Saul to be born a Roman citizen. See also Bargil Pixner, *The Fifth Gospel: With Jesus Through Galilee* (Rosh Pina, Israel: Corazin Publishing, 1992), 76.

3. This was apparently a "rabbi-disciple" relationship as the text (NRSV) literally says, "brought up in this city at the feet of Gamaliel," which is the Jewish phrase used for such training. While it is impossible to assign exact dates for this study, a boy usually began rabbinic training at about age twelve (for Paul, 6 AD) and studied until he was thirty (30 AD).

4. Luke's account in Acts ends with Paul in prison in Rome. However, church tradition holds that Paul was released after his first imprisonment and continued to teach the good news of Jesus. Events after his imprisonment are inferred by hints in Paul's pastoral letters (see Romans 15:28). It is likely Paul was arrested again and executed during Nero's persecution.

Session 1: Engaging the Mind: Paul in the Stoa of Athens

1. Acts 17:13–15.
2. For additional information, see "The Apostle Paul: A Time Line for His Life and Ministry" on pages 20–21. Also see That the World May Know, Vol. 15, *A Clash of Kingdoms*, session 1, pages 47–49.
3. R. E. Wycherley, "St. Paul at Athens," *Journal of Theological Studies*, 19:2 (1968): 619.
4. Deuteronomy 9:18–19.
5. Genesis 3:1–5.
6. For further study on the conflict of kingdoms see That the World May Know, Vol. 15, *A Clash of Kingdoms*, session 3, 139ff.
7. Christopher J. H. Wright, *The Mission of God* (Downers Grove, Ill.: InterVarsity Press, 2006). For an excellent discussion of the nature of pagan gods, see chapter "The Living God Confronts Idolatry."
8. 1 Corinthians 10:20.
9. Romans 1:5; 16:26.
10. Philippians 2:15; 1 Thessalonians 4:11–12; Titus 2:9–10.
11. Wright, *The Mission of God*, chapter 5.
12. Deuteronomy 4:15–19. In the context of forbidding idolatry, Moses warns Israel not to be enticed by them.
13. The Bible uses different Greek words having basically the same meaning: *Phoboumenos ton Theon* and *Seboumenos*

ton Theon, which mean the same as the title on the pillar: "God-fearing person." See J. Reynolds and R. Tannenbaum, *Jews and God-fearers at Aphrodisias: Greek Inscriptions with Commentary*, Proceedings of the Cambridge Philological Association Supp.12 (Cambridge Philological Society, 1987).

14. Romans 12:1–3.

15. Joseph A. Fitzmyer, *The Acts of the Apostles*, The Anchor Bible Commentary Series (New York: Doubleday, 1997), 604ff; Ben Witherington, *The Acts of the Apostles: A Socio-Rhetorical Commentary* (Grand Rapids: Eerdmans, 1998), 514.

16. Ibid.

Session 2: Engaging the Heart: Paul Before the Areopagus

1. 1 Peter 2:4–9.

2. Isaiah 42:8.

3. Acts 17:19–20.

4. Acts 18:12.

5. Romans 1:16.

6. Acts 19:32–28, 35–41.

7. Acts 14:8–18.

8. Ben Witherington, *The Acts of the Apostles: A Socio-Rhetorical Commentary* (Grand Rapids: Eerdmans, 1998), 521–524.

9. Hilary LeCornu, *The Jewish Roots of Acts*, Vol. 2 (Jerusalem: Academon, 2003), 960.

10. Ben Witherington, *New Testament History: A Narrative Account* (Grand Rapids: Baker, 2001), 268.

11. LeCornu, *The Jewish Roots of Acts*, Vol. 2, 960.

12. *Cultural Backgrounds Study Bible*, NIV (Grand Rapids: Zondervan, 2016). See comment on Acts 17:23.

13. For further discussion of Paul's early preparation, see That the World May Know, Vol. 7, *Walk as Jesus Walked*, session 2.

14. Acts 7:48. For the full story see Acts 6:8–8:3.

15. 2 Chronicles 6:18.

16. Isaiah 66:1–2.

17. Acts 7:48.

18. Psalm 44:18.

19. Psalm 119:101.

20. Numbers 14:18.

21. Jonah 4:2.

22. Acts 17:31–32.

23. Aeschylus, *Eumenides*, 644ff. Can be found online, for example: http://www.theoi.com/Text/AeschylusEumenides.html.

24. Witherington, *The Acts of the Apostles: A Socio-Rhetorical Commentary*, 533.

Session 3: Turning Weakness into Strength

1. 1 Corinthians 2:1–5.

2. For further background on Timothy as Paul's disciple, see That the World May Know, Vol. 7, *Walk as Jesus Walked*, session 3.

3. Ephesus, on the other side of the Aegean Sea, was a similar crossroads city. It was the terminal end of the ancient Royal Road. From Ephesus, we know that the gospel message reached all of the province of Asia (see Acts 19:8–10). Perhaps Paul chose Corinth and Ephesus as his ministry locations for more than four years because the gospel message could spread widely from both cities.

4. 1 Corinthians 1:27.

5. 2 Corinthians 13:4.

6. Ben Witherington, *The Acts of the Apostles: A Socio-Rhetorical Commentary* (Grand Rapids: Eerdmans, 1998), 545.

7. Suetonius, *Life of Claudius*, 25.4. Several translations are available online. Claudius (10 BC–54 AD) became emperor

in 41 AD after the assassination of Caligula. Hated by many, he depended on the legions to keep him in power. He was known to support the Jewish communities in the empire and issued edicts commanding tolerance of Jews and their unique practices. But around 48 AD riots broke out in Rome that were caused by disagreements among the large Jewish community over a certain "Chrestus." Some believe the conflict was over whether Jesus was the Christ (Messiah in Hebrew).

8. See 1 Corinthians 1:16; 16:15. It is certain Priscilla and Aquila were believers before meeting Paul because he considered Stephanas, whom he baptized in Corinth after he met Priscilla and Aquila, to be the first to join the Jesus movement in Corinth.

9. 1 Corinthians 2:1–2.

10. For further study on Timothy, see That the World May Know, Vol. 7, *Walk as Jesus Walked*, session 3, 85–120.

11. Philippians 2:22.

12. Acts 15:32.

13. Acts 18:5.

14. Just as there are multiple English translations of the New Testament, there are multiple Greek texts as well. The Western text usually is not considered to be the most accurate to the original (which we do not have, of course), but it often contains historically reliable material.

15. Hilary LeCornu, *The Jewish Roots of Acts*, Vol. 2 (Jerusalem: Academon, 2003), 992. Also F. F. Bruce, *New Testament History* (New York: Anchor, 1972), 315.

16. Acts 18:8.

17. Nehemiah 5:13.

18. Matthew 10:14; Mark 6:11; Luke 9:1–5.

19. See Ezekiel 3:16–19; 33:4.

20. James S. Jeffers, *The Greco-Roman World of the New Testament Era* (Downers Grove, Ill.: InterVarsity Press, 1999), 165.

21. 1 Kings 19:4. Refer to 1 Kings 17–19 for the full story of Elijah and King Ahab and Jezebel.

22. Deuteronomy 7:1–12.

23. 1 Corinthians 1:26–29.

24. LeCornu, *The Jewish Roots of Acts*, Vol. 2, 982.

25. The *agoranomos* was a powerful elected official with the responsibility and authority to ensure the legal operation of the agora, the commercial marketplace in ancient Greek cities.

26. Ben Witherington, *A Week in the Life of Corinth* (Downers Grove, Ill.: InterVarsity Press, 2012). Insightful historical fiction about Paul's visit to Corinth.

27. 2 Corinthians 13:4.

28. 1 Corinthians 4:12; 2 Corinthians 11:27–30; 12:10.

29. 1 Corinthians 1:2.

30. Jerome Murphy-O'Connor, *St. Paul's Corinth* (Collegeville, Minn.: Liturgical Press, 2002), 178ff.

31. Acts 2:44–45.

32. For a more in-depth study of God's people as his temple, see That the World May Know, Vol. 14, *The Mission of Jesus*, session 5; also Vol. 6, *In the Dust of the Rabbi*, session 3.

Session 4: The Lord's Supper: Discerning the Body

1. Mark 4:30–32.

2. Matthew 28:19–20.

3. See Numbers 15:37–41; Deuteronomy 22:12.

4. See En-Gedi Resource Center, http://www.egrc.net, "Director's Article," June 2003, and "Biblical Dress: Tassels." See the Jewish Publication Society, *Commentary on Numbers*, by Jacob Milgrom, 1990, excursus 38 on tassels (Tsitsit). See also That the World May Know, Vol. 3, *Life and Ministry of the Messiah*, session 5.

5. Jerome Murphy-O'Connor, *St. Paul's Corinth* (Collegeville, Minn.: Liturgical Press, 2002), 201–218.

6. Timothy was Paul's first disciple in the Jewish sense of one who traveled everywhere with the rabbi.

7. Matthew 12:22–29. See also That the World May Know, Vol. 14, *The Mission of Jesus*, sessions 1 and 2.

8. One day's wages for a laborer was between two and four sesterces.

9. Ben Witherington, *Conflict and Community in Corinth: A Socio-Rhetorical Commentary on 1 and 2 Corinthians* (Grand Rapids: Eerdmans, 1995). Witherington has an excellent treatment of Roman banquet customs and their relationship to Paul's instruction.

10. Sophocles, *Antigone*.

11. Jeffers, *The Greco-Roman World of the New Testament Era*, chapter 8.

12. For further study, please refer to That the World May Know, Vol. 5, *Early Church*, session 3, 83ff.

13. Murphy-O'Connor, *St. Paul's Corinth*, 186–191.

14. I found the following sources to be most helpful: Jerome Murphy-O'Connor, *St. Paul's Corinth*, part 3; Ben Witherington, *The Acts of the Apostles: A Socio-Rhetorical Commentary*, Argument VII; Wayne Meeks, *The First Urban Christians: The Social World of the Apostle Paul* (New Haven: Yale University Press, 1983.

15. Kenneth Bailey, *Paul Through Mediterranean Eyes: Cultural Studies in 1 Corinthians* (Downers Grove, Ill.: InterVarsity Press, 2011), chapter 4.4.

16. 1 Corinthians 1:10.

17. For helpful insight into the meaning of Paul's command "to discern the body," see Jeffrey A. D. Weima, "Children at the Lord's Supper and the Key Text of 1 Corinthians 11:17–34," in *Calvin Theological Seminary Forum*, Spring 2007, 7–9.

Session 5: Transforming the Chaos

1. Merrill C. Tenney, *New Testament Times* (Grand Rapids: Eerdmans, 1965), 273.

2. 1 Corinthians 6:12.

3. Matthew 28:19–20.

4. Leviticus 19:2. See also Baruch A. Levine, *The JPS Torah Commentary: Leviticus* (Philadelphia: Jewish Publication Society, 1989), Excursus #6.

5. 1 John 2:6.

6. 1 Corinthians 11:1.

7. Matthew 8:5–13.

8. Mark 7:24–30.

9. Mark 7:31–37.

10. Mark 15:39.

11. John Dominic Crossan and Jonathan L. Reed, *In Search of Paul* (San Francisco: Harper, 2004), 45.

12. *Antiquities* (XIV. x. 4).

13. 1 Maccabees 15.

14. 1 Samuel 17:46.

ACKNOWLEDGMENTS

The production of this study series is the work of a community of people. Many contributed their time and talent to make it possible. Recognizing the work of that unseen community is to me an important confirmation that we have learned the lessons God has been teaching his people for more than three thousand years. Here are the people God has used to make this study possible.

The Prince Foundation:

The vision of Elsa and Ed Prince—that this project that began in 1993 would enable thousands of people around the world to walk in the footsteps of the people of God—has never waned. God continues to use Elsa's commitment to share God's story with our broken world.

Focus on the Family:

Bob DeMoss—vice president, content development

Steve Johnson—associate publisher

Mitchell Wright—executive producer, visual media

Erin Berriman—director, ops & integration, visual media

Christi Lynn—director, product marketing

Allison Montjoy—manager, product marketing

Kay Leavy—senior coordinator, resource marketing

Zondervan:

John Raymond—vice president and publisher, curriculum

Beth Murphy—senior director, curriculum marketing and sales

T. J. Rathbun—director, audio/visual production

Belinda Bass—art director

Ben Fetterley, Denise Froehlich—book interior designers

Greg Clouse—production editor

That the World May Know:

Chris Hayden—research assistant. This series would not have been completed nor would it have the excellence of content it has without his outstanding research effort.

Lois Tverberg, PhD

Nadav Hillebrand

Alison Elders

Lisa Fredricks

Kostas Kolizeras, PhD

Grooters Productions:

John Grooters—producer/director

Judy Grooters—producer

Mark Chamberlin—director of photography

Mark Chamberlin, John Grooters, Adam Vardy, Tyler Jackson—cinematography

Alan Arroyo—assistant editor

Paul Wesselink—re-recording mixer and sound design

Carlos Martinez—orchestrations

Brittany Grooters, Jordyn Osburn, Hannah Dozeman, Hollie Noble—post-production assistants

Dave Lassanske, Shawn Kamerman, Eric Schrotenboer, Kate Chamberlin—camera assistants

Paul Wesselink, Ryan Wert—production sound

Dennis Lassanske, Alan Arroyo, Brittany Grooters, Taylor Wogoman, Hannah Dozeman, Nola Tolsma—production support

Taylor Wogoman—motion graphics

Breana Melvin, Charlie Shaw, Rob Perry, John Walker, Drew Johnson—illustrators

Eric Schrotenboer—music

Sorenson Communications:

Stephen and Amanda Sorenson—writers

BIBLIOGRAPHY

Bailey, Kenneth E. *Jacob and the Prodigal*. Downers Grove, Ill.: IVP Academic, 2003.

_____. *Paul Through Mediterranean Eyes*. Downers Grove, Ill.: IVP Academic, 2008.

Bauckham, Richard, ed. *The Book of Acts in Its Palestinian Setting*, vol 4. Grand Rapids: Eerdmans, 1995.

Beitzel, Barry J. *Moody Bible Atlas*. Chicago: Moody Press, 1985.

Berlin, Adele, and Marc Zvi Brettler. *Jewish Study Bible*. Philadelphia: Jewish Publication Society and New York: Oxford University Press, 2004.

Bivin, David. *New Light on the Difficult Words of Jesus: Insights from His Jewish Context*. Holland, Mich.: EnGedi Resource Center, 2005. (www.egrc.net)

Bruce, F. F. *New Testament History*. New York: Anchor Books, 1972.

Crossan, John Dominic, and Jonathan L. Reed. *In Search of Paul*. San Francisco: Harper, 2004.

Danby, Herbert. *The Mishnah*. New York: Oxford University Press, 1977, Sanhedrin 4.5.

Evans, Craig A. "Mark's Incipit and the Priene Calendar Inscription: From Jewish Gospel to Greco-Roman Gospel," *Journal of Greco-Roman Christianity and Judaism* 1 (2000), 67–81. (http://www.craigaevans.com/studies.htm.)

First International Congress on Antioch of Pisidia: A Collection of Scholarly Papers. Yalvac, Turkey: Kocaeli Publishers, 1997.

Fitzmyer, Joseph, A. *The Acts of the Apostles*, The Anchor Bible Commentary. New York: Doubleday, 1998.

Garnsey, Peter. *Social Status and Legal Privilege in the Roman Empire*. Clarendon, England: Oxford Press, 1970.

Gill, David W. J., and Conrad Gempf. *The Book of Acts in Its First Century Setting: The Book of Acts in Its Graeco-Roman Setting*, vol. 2. Grand Rapids: Eerdmans, 1994.

Green, Gene L., *The Pillar New Testament Commentary: Letters to the Thessalonians*. Grand Rapids: Eerdmans, 2002.

Hillers, Delbert R. *Covenant: The History of a Biblical Idea*. Baltimore: Johns Hopkins Press, 1969.

Howard-Brook, Wes. *Come Out My People!* Maryknoll, N.Y.: Orbis Books, 2011.

Jeffers, James S. *The Greco-Roman World of the New Testament Era*. Downers Grove, Ill.: IVP Academic, 1999.

LeCornu, Hilary. *The Jewish Roots of Acts*, vols. 1 and 2. Jerusalem: Academon, 2003.

Levine, Amy-Jill, and Marc Zvi Brettler. *The Jewish Annotated New Testament*. New York: Oxford University Press, 2011.

Levine, Baruch A. *The JPS Torah Commentary: Leviticus*. Philadelphia: Jewish Publication Society, 1989.

Levinskaya, Irina. *The Book of Acts in Its First Century Setting: Diaspora Setting*, vol. 5. Grand Rapids: Eerdmans, 1994.

McRay, John. *Paul: His Life and Teaching*. Grand Rapids: Baker Academics, 2004.

Meeks, Wayne. *The First Urban Christians: The Social World of the Apostle Paul*. New Haven: Yale University Press, 1983.

Murphy-O'Connor, Jerome, *St. Paul's Corinth*. Collegeville, Minn.: Liturgical Press, 2002.

Notley, Steven R., and Ze'ev Safrai. *Parables of the Sages*. Jerusalem: Carta, 2011.

Osiek, Carolyn, and David L. Balch. *Families in the New Testament World: Households and House Churches*. Louisville: John Knox Press, 1997.

Pixner, Bargil. *With Jesus Through Galilee According to the Fifth Gospel*. Rosh Pina, Israel: Corazin Publishing, 1992.

Pryor, Dwight A. *Unveiling the Kingdom of Heaven*. Dayton, Ohio: Center for Judaic Christian Studies, 2008. www.jcstudies.com.

Rainey, Anson F. and R. Steven Notley. *The Sacred Bridge: Carta's Atlas of the Biblical World*. Jerusalem: Carta, 2007, page 360.

Rapske, Brian. *The Book of Acts in Its First Century Setting: Paul in Roman Custody*. Grand Rapids: Eerdmans, 1994.

Richter, Sandra L. *The Epic of Eden*. Downers Grove, Ill.: IVP Academic, 2008.

Ryken, Leland, James C. Wilhoit, and Tremper Longman III. *Dictionary of Biblical Imagery*. Downers Grove, Ill.: IVP Academic, 1998.

Sacks, Rabbi Jonathan. *To Heal a Fractured World: The Ethics of Responsibility*. New York: Schocken Books, 2005.

Safrai, S., and M. Stern. *The Jewish People in the First Century*. Amsterdam: Van Gorcum, 1976.

Santala, Risto. *Paul: The Man and the Teacher*. Jerusalem: Keren Ahvah Meshihit, 1995.

Schowalter, Daniel N., and Steven J. Friesen. *Urban Religion in Roman Corinth*. Cambridge: Harvard Theological Studies, 2005.

Taylor, Lily Ross. *The Divinity of the Emperor*. Middletown, Conn.: Scholars Press, 1931.

Telushkin, Rabbi Joseph. *The Book of Jewish Values*. New York: Bell Tower Publishers, 2000, 70.

Tenney, Merrill C. *New Testament Survey*. Grand Rapids: Eerdmans, 1961.

Tverberg, Lois. *Reading the Bible with Rabbi Jesus*. Grand Rapids: Zondervan, 2018.

_____. *Walking in the Dust of Rabbi Jesus*. Grand Rapids: Zondervan, 2012.

Tverberg, Lois, with Bruce Okkema. *Listening to the Language of the Bible*. Holland, Mich.: En Gedi Resource Center, 2004. (www.egrc.net)

Tverberg, Lois, and Ann Spangler. *Sitting at the Feet of Rabbi Jesus*. Grand Rapids: Zondervan, 2009.

Whiston, William, trans. *Flavius Josephus: The Jewish War. VII. 3–7*. Complete works of Josephus.

_____. *Josephus: Complete Works, Antiquities*, 10.14.25. See Josephus, *Josephus: Complete Works*, (1867) reprint. Grand Rapids: Kregel, 1972.

White, Michael I. *Building God's House in the Roman World*. Baltimore: Johns Hopkins University, 1990.

Wilson, Mark. "In the Footsteps of Paul in Asia Minor: Are There Still Roman Roads Left to Follow?" *Biblical Archaeology Society Lecture Series,* Fest XII—Part 2. Washington, D.C., 2010.

Wilson, Marvin R. *Exploring our Hebraic Heritage*. Grand Rapids: Eerdmans, 2014.

_____. *Our Father Abraham: The Jewish Roots of the Christian Faith*. Grand Rapids: Eerdmans, 2014. See especially chapters 1 and 8.

Witherington, Ben. *Conflict and Community in Corinth: A Socio-Rhetorical Commentary on 1 and 2 Corinthians*. Grand Rapids: Eerdmans, 1995.

_____. *Friendship and Finances in Philippi*. Valley Forge, Pa.: Trinity Press International, 1994.

_____. *New Testament History*. Grand Rapids: Baker, 2001.

_____. *The Acts of the Apostles: A Socio-Rhetorical Commentary*. Grand Rapids: Eerdmans, 1998.

_____. *A Week in the Life of Corinth*. Downers Grove, Ill.: IVP Academic, 2012.

Worth, Roland H. *The Seven Cities of the Apocalypse and Roman Culture*. New York: Paulist Press, 1999.

Wright, Christopher J. H. *The Mission of God*. Downers Grove, Ill.: IVP Academic, 2006.

Wright, N. T. "Paul, Arabia, and Elijah: Galatians 1:17." *Journal of Biblical Literature*, vol. 115, 683–692.

_____. *Simply Jesus: A New Vision of Who He Was, What He Did, and Why He Matters*. New York: Harper Collins, 2011.

Wu, Jackson. *One Gospel for All Nations*. Pasadena: William Carey Library, 2015.

Yamauchi, Edwin. *Harper's World of the New Testament*. San Francisco: Harper and Row, 1981.

Young, Brad H. *The Parables: Jewish Tradition and Christian Interpretation*. Peabody, Mass.: Hendrickson Publishers, 1998.

More Great Resources
from Focus on the Family ®

Volume 1: Promised Land
Learn about the nation of ancient Israel, God's purpose for his people, and why he placed them in the Promised Land.

Volume 2: Prophets and Kings
Learn about the nation of Israel during Old Testament times to understand how the people struggled with the call of God to be separate and holy nation.

Volume 3: Life and Ministry of the Messiah
Explore the life and teaching ministry of Jesus and discover new insights about the Son of God.

Volume 4: Death and Resurrection the Messiah
Witness the passion of the Messiah as he resolutely sets his face toward Jerusalem to suffer and die for his bride.

Volume 5: The Early Church
Capture the fire of the early church and see how the first Christians lived out their faith.

Volume 6: In the Dust of the Rabbi
Discover how to follow Jesus as you walk with Ray Vander Laan through the breathtaking terrains of Israel and Turkey.

Volume 7: Walk as Jesus Walked
Journey to Israel where the 12 disciples walk the walk their rabbi Jesus taught them.

Volume 8: God Heard Their Cry
Join Ray Vander Laan in ancient Egypt for his study of God's faithfulness to the Israelites—a promise that remains true today.

Volume 9: Fire on the Mountain
Discover how God teaches the Israelites (and us) what it means to be part of a community that loves him.

Volume 10: With All Your Heart
In this volume, you'll learn how quickly the Israelites forgot God after they entered the Promised Land. Do you remember where your blessings come from?

Volume 11: The Path to the Cross

Discover how the Israelites' passionate faith prepares the way for Jesus, and be challenged to live as they did—by every word that comes from the mouth of God.

Volume 12: Walking with God in the Desert

During difficult times, it's easy to think God has disappeared. Instead, discover that it's only when we're totally dependent on God that we find him closer than ever.

Volume 13: Israel's Mission

God gave the assignment to his people thousands of years ago: to bring "lost sheep" back into his kingdom. And it's still our task today. Discover the mission that can give your life greater meaning than you ever imagined.

Volume 14: The Mission of Jesus

In John 17:26 Jesus says: "I made known your name to them, and I will continue to make it known." Discover how Jesus triumphantly made God's presence known on earth, and how he asks you to do the same—bringing God's shalom to the chaos of others.

Volume 15: A Clash of Kingdoms

As Christians, we're called to proclaim God's name in all the earth, but how do we do that in the midst of false gospels? In this volume, discover how Paul communicated the good news of Christ to Philippi, a Roman colony that worshiped false gods. Can you live the message as Paul did while he encouraged the church in Philippi to consider itself a colony of heaven, not Rome? Consider your citizenship—and the message you convey to the world—as Ray Vander Laan takes you deeper into the culture of ancient Philippi.

FOCUS ON THE FAMILY®

Online: Go to ThatTheWorldMayKnow.com

Phone: Call toll-free: 800-A-FAMILY (232-6459)

In Canada, call toll-free: 800-661-9800